Bikini Is a State of Mind

Nancy Gardner, Ann Haley,
Cynthia Lewis, and Lina Soares

1663 LIBERTY DRIVE, SUITE 200
BLOOMINGTON, INDIANA 47403
(800) 839-8640
WWW.AUTHORHOUSE.COM

First published by AuthorHouse 2/1/2006

ISBN: 1-4208-9750-0 (sc)

Library of Congress Control Number: 2005910256

Printed in the United States of America
Bloomington, Indiana

This book is printed on acid-free paper.

Dedicated to "Big Lina"

*bikini [French, from **Bikini,** atoll of the Marshall Islands, 1947]: a woman's scanty two-piece bathing suit*

1

Without our friends and supporters, we might still be a team, but we wouldn't have produced this book. Our thanks to Cary Wade for her recipes and to Jane and Bobby Avinger, Elizabeth Bradford, Amy Edwards, Jay Everette, Bill Giduz, Beth Helfrich, Meg Kimmel, and Liz Pierce, all of whom are to be found in and between the lines.

Chapter 1:
Bikini as a
State of Mind

Bikini Ethos

"It is not if you can. It is if you will." With these words, esteemed Bikini Team CEO, the Serene Miss Haley, captures the essence of Bikini and membership on the Bikini Team. How? By implying that the courage to wear a bikini comes from within and has nothing to do with looking flawless in the team uniform. Who among us looks perfect in a bikini? A handful of teenagers and, on our team, only Nancy Gardner. And that's a moot point. No, wearing a bikini and proudly belonging to the Bikini Team don't require a perfect appearance, but a joyful self-acceptance and an understanding of the fact that, again in the wise words of our CEO, "Bikini is a state of mind."

What kind of state, exactly? Let's begin with yourself. Do you feel as if you work so hard most of the time that any pampering you allow yourself in return is richly—indeed, unquestionably—deserved? If so, you are on your way. Do you feel that a tan, however acquired, is the one ingredient of your summer that you would never go without? Would you rather be tanning, lounging around a pool with your teammates, and exchanging all manner of trivialities than be shaded at home, between the hours of 1:00 and 3:00, baking a cherry pie? Do you find yourself thinking a good deal of the time about manicures, pedicures, massages, naps, and fine dining outside the home? Do you have wit enough to wear your bikini under your work clothes, thus allowing for disrobing and tanning on a moment's notice? Do you keep your float in your car at all times—inflated—ever prepared for even a few minutes on the water? Is buying next season's swimsuit high on your list of seasonal priorities and a source of intense excitement? Do you find yourself trying on swimsuits at all times of the year, fantasizing about when you will be wearing one again? And, when you look at yourself in the mirror wearing one of those suits and wonder how you could possibly be three months pregnant at age fifty-one, do you shrug off your imperfections and keep Bikini foremost in your thoughts? If you answered "yes" to all or most of these questions, you too are a likely candidate for membership on a Bikini Team.

Now to the team itself. You'll need a critical mass (but not too massive) of like-minded sisters who enjoy socializing with one another enough to while away afternoons at the pool, evenings at happy hour, mornings in a coffee shop, and long weekends on retreats. (The authors of this book cannot stress enough the importance of light-hearted camaraderie among team members. Over-seriousness is anathema and should be expunged at the earliest detection. For more information on the subject of insufferable seriousness, see Chapter 6 on PITAs.) You should proceed carefully in assembling your group, since this team is likely to outlast most members' marriages. Have you gathered together women who share such interests as make-up, gossip, health tips, and travel? Do these women keep talk about their children to an essential minimum? Do they consider themselves much funnier than they actually are? (Remember, you will often be laughing uproariously at the pool and elsewhere about nothing at all.) Are they open about their feelings, their trials, their passions, their shoe wardrobe? Do they know which details to include and which to omit about their visits to the gynecologist?

We'd like to be clear from the start that we, like all women who have reached their '50s, have met with personal trauma and suffered considerable set-backs, including ugly divorces and the death of a spouse. None of us makes a great deal of money, and we all have to pinch pennies every day of the year. No matter how frivolous we may sometimes seem, no matter how much pampering we may indulge ourselves, no matter how luxurious our summer existence may appear, we've made a conscious choice to counter our troubles— family, monetary, career, and personal—with the joyous treat every summer of stealing a few hours a day for ourselves. We aren't doing a single thing that any woman can't do if she wants to. Nor does she have to do it with bikinis. Yes, our manifesto is that wearing a bikini is an act of self-acceptance available to each and every woman. But other women will find or tailor their own means of expressing and realizing their freedom from what other people think. Our way is but one way, and it is a metaphor. In this book, we won't dwell on the problems we're dealing with, and we'll assume our readers are dealing with plenty themselves. We'll move on to what we do to cope, have some fun, and hope that our readers will seek out their own version of doing just that. Plant your tongue in your cheek—or at least attune your ear to hearing our self-irony—and forge ahead!

The best Bikini Teams are formed organically, over time, like ours in Davidson, North Carolina. We belong to the Swimming Hole, a private swimming pool without the usual amenities of one (like a good diving board or a snack bar). Today, the team numbers five: Nancy Gardner, Ann Haley, Cynthia Lewis, Lina Soares, and Cary Wade. But a vital team is always evolving, occasionally losing a member and, less frequently, gaining a member. Nancy's and Lina's families were founders of the Swimming Hole, which opened in 1960, when they were seven. The Serene Miss Haley's aunt and uncle joined the pool when the girls were young. Friendship among these women has flourished for decades. New friendships have formed over the years with women who have moved to town, paid their dues in the baby pool, and naturally gravitated to the spirited women on the team.

We consider our founder Lina's aunt—"Big Lina," as we reverently call her, although, at eighty-two years of age, she is five feet tall, weighs ninety-five pounds, and wears a size 0. Big Lina—Lina Adams Bell—is our inspiration because, as her niece says of her, "She was ahead of the women's liberation movement. She has always been avant-garde." She never married any of her boyfriends, lived for many years on Spain's Costa del Sol, and became one of the Flying Tigers, at that time a group of commercial airplane pilots. She went to Hong Kong to have her diminutive wardrobe made and has always taken meticulous care with her physical appearance. Those of us with a place on the current team strive to follow her independent example, although her tiny shoes are difficult to fill.

Her swimming attire, however, was the focus for four little girls when Big Lina flew into town from California for a visit and landed at the Swimming Hole, wearing, of all things, a bikini. All parties present at the time report that she was eye-catching, whether sporting the red and white bikini that showcased her tan or her classic navy and white polka dot number. The girls, nine or ten back then, were at the pool to swim the day away; they wore sensible Catalina tank suits in non-fading dark blue and black. But the image of Big Lina in those itsy-bitsy-teeny-weenies not only made a big splash with those impressionable girls, but also had a long-lasting effect.

Today, Big Lina exemplifies the spirit of the women on the Davidson team—hard-working professionals and loving mothers who guard their freedom jealously. All of our members are teachers—some in public school systems, one at the local YMCA, and one at the college level. (Note: A teaching career need not be a pre-requisite for membership on any Bikini Team.) All but one of us have seen our fiftieth birthday come and go. (Cary is a forty-something.) We are middle-generation "It" girls, each with interests in addition to what she does for a living. One is pursuing her Ph.D.; another is a national consultant for the senior project in public schools; yet another writes professionally. Nearly every member has received teaching awards. Several have earned their National Board Certification as public school teachers. We all get along well because we respect one another for these and other accomplishments, but also because we know how to ignore them. We understand that our external achievements pale in importance to being caring mothers, invested friends, eternal goddesses, and wild women. What we love most is not high achievement, but being released in the summer to spend our time as we want: goofing around.

As you recruit for your very own team, remember that some of the most promising potential members have obstacles to surmount. Be understanding and proceed with care. Cynthia, the newest Davidson member, took considerable coaxing before she would even wear a bikini (see information on the Bikini Adaptor Kit™, Chapter 8). Her example is helpful to keep in mind lest you begin to despair that a prospective member simply can't be coached. Dabbling one evening in a department store dressing room, a year before she was ready to appear publicly in her uniform, she called her mother in to look at a sale bikini she was trying on. (Note: be wary of sale bikinis; they almost never fit as well as they might.) Her confused seven-year-old son thought he was invited in too, and, at the sight of his mother in a bikini—stark white stomach and all—ran out of the dressing room clutching his head and screaming, "No! Not *my* mother! Not *my* mother, too!" But all's well that ends well. The child soon recovered and, thereafter, was able to accept his mother as a viable team member. One spring day many months later, having finally acquired her first bikini, Cynthia was wearing her top outside while gardening. Cary spotted her and reported to the rest of the team that she'd sighted Cynthia "out practicing." Now converted, Cynthia is never going back to a one-piece and considers herself a teammate for life. She has won the "Rookie of the Year" award for three consecutive years.

Team versus Club

Davidson Bikini Team members often hear themselves referred to erroneously as a "club." They try to correct this gaffe gently and politely: "Excuse me, but we're really a team" or "I'm sure you meant to say *team*, not *club*." Despite the often considerable embarrassment elicited, the public is generally gratified to learn of this distinction and grateful for instruction.

But, you may well ask, why *team* and not *club*? In essence, because Bikini is a sport. We consider our exertions in behalf of Bikini to be as rigorous, all-consuming, dedicated, and, yes, physically engaging as those of any athletic team. Put another way, we on the Davidson Bikini Team work as hard at relaxing as any world class champion does in his or her sports category.

Team members are often queried at the pool about their athletic prowess and purposes. As one little girl asked of a team member who had fallen asleep on her float, "Do you ever swim? Or do you just lie there all day?" Gathering her wits upon being awakened, the member replied to the darling little girl, "No, dear, swimming is for amateur athletes. I'm tanning."

Team solidarity, as important to Bikini as to any serious sport, depends not only on wearing the team uniform, but also on holding daily meetings at the pool. We've agreed to attend our meetings promptly between the hours of 11:00 and 4:00, when we take up matters of crucial importance. Do tankinis qualify as official team uniforms? (no.) Should we support the women life guards in their quest to wear two-piece suits, rather than tank suits? (yes.) Will we be bringing chardonnay tomorrow in our water bottles? (most certainly.) When the harsh North Carolina heat prohibits meeting on the concrete, in lounge chairs, we launch our floats in the pool. There in the cool water, our heads cleared from the unbearable heat, we hatch brilliant strategies—like midnight skinny dipping. The festive colors of our floats not only make a fashion statement, but also come together to form a giant "tanning bed" that children enjoy swimming under. (It *is* difficult to get around.)

Appreciating that, lying on our backs, we would be inconvenienced if forced to get our *own* popsicles, the devoted life guards bring each of us whichever flavor we request. They even peel off the wrappers and hand the icy treats directly to us. This, we believe, is team work.

Group projects also help to further team spirit and unity. One of our most successful enterprises has been the Bikini Team calendar. We bribe one of our favorite photographers with a zucchini cobbler or fresh tomato pie to undertake a photo shoot. Each member helps design the page for her month, adopting an appropriate nickname for her calendar identity: Nanci, Cindi, Lina Bell, Granny. Several months feature group photos. Shots are, of course, made in the team uniform. We take the finished product to Kinko's and have a very limited number of copies made, thus rendering the calendar one of the most coveted items in the county at year's beginning. We have yet to grace the walls of any local gas stations that we know of, but we are guessing that Wayne Stowe will display one in his Exxon station if we give one to him this year (see Chapter 9,

"The Bikini Male"). We suspect, furthermore, that a couple of missing calendars have found their way into appreciative hands. In any event, the team finds the pictures and the exercise of assembling them endlessly amusing.

We also relish brainstorming about entrepreneurial schemes that our team might pursue. Just last year, we hit upon the ingenious idea of marketing official Bikini Team dolls à la Barbie. While our effigies might not match the shapeliness of Barbie and her cohorts, we feel sure that any little girl would be proud to own a Bikini Team likeness—whether sultry Cynthia, petite Nancy, or Lina, the Doris Day look-alike. What's more, the possibilities for accessorizing are infinite—designer water bottles, sequined sun glasses, an array of colorful inner tubes and floats, flip flops to complement every bikini and sarong . . . just like real life!

Members versus Wannabes

Not surprisingly, the Bikini Team has inspired no little envy at the Swimming Hole and even in the wider community. This is partly because we have the chutzpah to wear bikinis—but only partly. Equally important, Bikini envy stems from the team's conspicuous poolside fun. "Boy, I'd like to move over to your corner," says one on-looker. "You guys are having a riot over there," says another. "What's your secret?" No secret, just inanity. That we all have loud belly laughs further encourages others to look on with envy and to wonder what could possibly be so funny. Yet another woman recently confided to a member, "One day when ya'll weren't there, I sat in your spot, and it felt wonderful!"

Now, we on the team realize that we may seem exclusive and snobbish. But that is not our intent in circling our lounge chairs every day in the same corner of the pool and in the same configuration. We must put our chairs close together, in a row, to be able to hear one another gossip and joke, and we must position all chairs for optimal exposure to the afternoon sun. (Note: We are aware of the dangers of sunlight and take many precautions—sun screen, hats, and sun glasses—to guard against its most ravaging effects.) From the outside looking in, however, we no doubt appear clique-ish, as if we were claiming ownership of that one corner. Anyone else who ventures to sit there before a team member arrives is either new to pool membership or brazenly trying her (or his) hand at interloping. On occasion, a Bikini Team member will arrive at the pool to find a cheeky non-member or two in our space. "We're sitting in your spot!" they exclaim, beaming. Team members' responses to such bravado vary: "So you are." "Good for you." "As long as you're here, do you have any chardonnay on you?"

Such confrontation on the part of non-members is the mark of wannabes. If they can't join us, they want to beat us. But most would rather join us, the *enfants terribles* of the pool scene. We are solicited constantly. Our favor is curried daily. We are flattered by this desire to belong, and we agree that we have a good thing going. We understand our own appeal. But, like the neighborhood that is desirable only while others desire it, but don't occupy it, our group works because it is small and tight. We enjoy one another so much and have developed a level of intimacy so close that, most times, we can't imagine taking in a new member, however motivated. This is not snobbery. It is sisterhood.

That being said, a few guidelines for expressing interest in a Bikini Team may help the serious candidate for membership further her cause:

-- When you tell Bikini Team members that you want to join their team, **don't** wear a one-piece suit (unless you can show proof of purchase of an official Bikini Adaptor Kit™) and **don't** make remarks like, "I'd love to be on your team, but I just couldn't wear a bikini." That's rather like saying you want to do weight training, but don't want muscles. The team uniform is the *sine qua non* of membership.

-- **Don't** tell team members you want to join their **club**.

-- **Do** offer to bring tomorrow's chardonnay in an appropriately festive water bottle.

-- **Do** rely on your sense of humor to connect you to the team. If you've temporarily lost it, find it ASAP. If you never had it, go to another corner.

-- If you are invited to a team get-together, **do** offer to bring a great deal of food, wine, and other welcome items, but **don't** use recipes from *Martha Stewart Living* or *Good Housekeeping.* Bikini Team members enjoy cooking and appreciate good food, but dislike pretentiousness and are uninterested in '50's nostalgia. (See team-approved recipes following various chapters.)

-- When you go out with members or help throw a party, **do** be sure to pay your fair share. The Bikini Team dislikes moochers.

-- **Do** be sure to notice new bikinis. Yours will be noticed in return.

-- **Don't** attempt to dominate conversation with the Bikini Team. Remember that all five members are already vying one another for air time; as many as three of them may be talking at once.

-- **Do** be sure to research individual members of the team. Who is in charge? (the CEO.) Who is responsible for bringing mail order catalogs—summer reading material—to team meetings? (the Media Specialist.) Who brings the snacks? (the Team Caterer.) Who tries, usually in vain, to keep members on the straight and narrow? (the Chaplain.) Who tells the funniest stories? (the Raconteur.) Who gives demerits? (the Sargeant-at-Arms.)

Guest Lecturers

Davidson, NC, a college town, is home to a wide range of experts on many topics, whether quantum mechanics, the economics of urban decline in Cleveland, or the relative merits of Lancôme, Clinique, and Mary Kay sun screen. Such experts make excellent guest lecturers at a Bikini Team meeting. They are honored by the invitation, and we, in return, are edified. It is a win-win situation. What's more, hosting guest lecturers mitigates the impression of the team's exclusivity. Far from snobs, we seek enlightenment and companionship outside of our small circle of lounge chairs. Guest lectureships are also a clever way of letting an attractive man know that somebody on the team wants him around the pool.

Guest lecturers often accompany Bikini Team members on outings. One of our favorites, an Italian Renaissance art historian, has not only filled us in on Tintoretto's contribution to the development of

Renaissance painting, but has also shown us how to navigate through the dense crowds of singles' night at Vinnie's Sardine Bar (on the local lake) without spilling wine on our summer frocks. Similarly, when Nancy's sister Mary Mig comes to town and goes out with us, we always learn a thing or two about karaoke. We're also reminded that, if it's a career in singing we're looking for, most of us had better not give up those pesky day jobs just yet. On occasion, a guest appearance goes awry, as when a friend, invited to speak about something as uplifting as choosing toe-less hosiery for open-toed shoes, winds up boring us with talk of our pesky day jobs. But such aberrations are, thankfully, rare.

While Bikini Team guests may include spouses (a dwindling breed), children (who learn to sit still at about college age), out-of-town friends (who find the Swimming Hole a regular tourist attraction), and curious locals, we are especially welcoming when any of those non-members agree to appear as guest lecturers. They broaden our horizons, stir our imagination, and show us new opportunities.

And, in case you're wondering, all guests are allowed to wear a one-piece suit.

Confidentiality

One word will suffice about protecting Bikini bonding and team spirit: secrecy. In respect to one another, team members are vaults. If one of us tells the others to keep a matter private, no one questions that even spouses will be kept in the dark. After all, we bond on the basis of shared trust and intimacy; to keep that bond sacred, we must be willing to swallow gossip that, otherwise, we'd disgorge with small provocation. For example, when team member A chose to experiment with Botox, she asked the team to keep it quiet. No problem. After member A's procedure, a third party remarked to team member B that team member A looked especially good. Team member B looked her straight in the eye and remarked about team member A, "She's been working with a personal trainer." Perfect.

Similarly, team members trust one another to avoid the dreaded word *school*. (This will be the last mention of that word in this text.) Yes, Bikini Team members are, by and large, some of the most dedicated teachers in the state of North Carolina. But enough is enough. The shortened summer vacations, the low pay, the cutbacks to health insurance (not to mention the cutbacks to educational programs themselves), and the legislature's lack of understanding about education take their toll. Good teachers need what little is left of their summer to unwind and to think about matters other than their jobs so that they can return in August feeling refreshed and renewed. That's why the Bikini Team has a rule against discussing "S" at meetings and even against using the "S word." Just "S" will do.

Demerits and Awards

While the Bikini Team is usually generous, forgiving, and tolerant, it is, at base, a meritocracy. That being the case, members are subject to demerits for various forms of aberrant behavior—most often, for poor attendance at meetings, social gatherings, or retreats. To date, demerits have remained a rather abstract concept; no one has suffered actual penalty or adversity from collecting a bushel load. In the future,

23

however, rare punishments may be devised for a member who is deemed by the group to stray too far afield of its goals and expectations. A teammate who talks too much about "S," for example, may have her float flipped over and her hair and make-up ruined.

By the same token, exceptional virtue is rewarded at our annual awards ceremony. Here, our esteemed CEO, the Serene Miss Haley, and our Sergeant-at-Arms, Nancy Gardner, recognize all manner of accomplishments from "Best Tan" to "Tight End" to "Most Sacks" to "Carpe Noctem" to the ever-coveted MVP, for which several players are each year known to be gunning. The immense pride members take in their awards is difficult to overstate. Some team members, however, suspect that the awards may be rigged, since the CEO and Sergeant-at-Arms have yet to go a year without sharing the MVP Award, and since the Big Lina Award* is a given. Such recognition makes all of the sacrifices, all of the difficult back work**, all of the spring training worthwhile.

*the Big Lina Award, according to CEO the Serene Miss Haley, is given to the person most like Big Lina in body, mind, spirit, and name. Little Lina has, thus far, never lost it.

**the difficult back work is Bikini jargon for the challenging process of tanning one's back, especially while pursuing various team pleasures like talking, laughing, and reading mail-order catalogs.

Recipes for Chapter 1

These are tried and true recipes that have been approved and enjoyed by the Bikini Team . . .

<u>TOMATO PIE</u>

Crust

2 cups Bisquick

2/3 cup milk

Mix together and press into bottom and up the sides of a large, greased deep-dish pie pan.

Filling

fresh tomatoes, sliced thin

green onions, chopped (whites too)

lots of fresh basil leaves, chopped

1/2 cup plain yogurt, drained of excess water through a coffee filter placed in a plastic cone

1/2 cup mayo

1 cup grated parmesan

Slice enough fresh tomatoes to fill the cavity. Layer tomatoes, onion, and basil in crust. Mix together yogurt, mayo, and cheese and pour on top of pie. Bake 30 minutes at 400 degrees. Let sit at least 15 minutes before cutting. (The longer it sits the better, since the juices will be absorbed into the crust.) Can be made ahead.

<u>LINABELLS</u>

1 small can of frozen limeade

1 can vodka

3 large peaches with skin

Place ingredients in a blender with ice cubes. Blend and drink to your satisfaction.

When peaches are not as sweet as we like, we add a splash of peach Schnapps. Shoot, why not add the schnapps anyway? Couldn't hurt!

<u>SEAFOOD BISQUE</u>

Make a roux using 3T butter, 3T flour. Stir often, cooking the flour, but not browning it (low to medium heat for 15-20 minutes). Keep the roux a creamy color. Mince an onion, two peppers (red or green), two cloves of garlic and 6 medium (or 3-4 large) tomatoes. (Use canned ones in winter). When the roux is ready, add the vegetables, beginning with the peppers, then add onions and garlic. Add tomatoes last, smashing the pulp with a fork while stirring often. The longer these flavors cook slowly and blend, the better. Cook for a minimum of 15 minutes. About 15 minutes before serving, move this mixture to a large pot. Add one or two bottles of clam juice, a pound or two of shellfish (minced), a quart of half and half, and your favorite blend of mustard, bay leaves, pepper, dill, and salt. You can also pulverize it in the food processor if you like a smooth bisque, or vary the texture based on how you chop the ingredients. It's good hot or cold.

Chapter 2:
The Bikini Team
Spring Training Regime

Training for a professional sport is an art, as well as a science. We on the Bikini Team are very serious about our Spring Training Regime. This program prepares us not only physically, but also emotionally and spiritually for the demanding summer season of tanning and relaxing.

The Spring Training Regime begins each year in January, almost five months before our first meeting on the opening day of the pool. Team members receive the Spring Training Regime via e-mail. We also receive gentle reminders and letters of encouragement periodically throughout the training season. It is the responsibility of each member to follow the program faithfully, to monitor herself, and to strive for her personal best.

The Spring Training Regime is a scientifically developed program with proven results. It is extremely precise and demanding. Team members must complete a series of ten steps each day. We give ourselves strength during the difficult training by visualizing our tanned, bikini-clad bodies floating on rafts in the pool. As we drift aimlessly, we eat our popsicles. This is Heaven.

As teachers, we fully understand the value of a comprehensive testing program. The Bikini Team Pre-Test is administered on January 6, Epiphany, before the Spring Training Regime begins. The Bikini Team Post-Test is given at the end of The Season, Labor Day. Pre- and Post-Test results are compared to determine the individual growth of each member. All test scores are kept completely confidential.

In this chapter you will find:

-- A letter of introduction to The Spring Training
   Regime
-- The Bikini Team Pre-Test
-- The Bikini Team Spring Training Regime
-- The Bikini Team Post-Test
-- Swim-Suit-Able Recipes

Letter of Introduction

Dearest Teammates,

Spring is in the air! It is now time to begin
our yearly journey, our noble crusade, indeed, our
eternal quest to reach au Pantheon.

Our goal is to attain the perfect harmony—
possible only when our hearts, minds, and bodies
are at their highest levels—the state of bliss known
only to the chosen, the elusive Nirvana.

This has been a difficult year, a year like no
other, but we will not succumb to fate. We will
prevail. The recent unpleasantness in the world
and at home has only made us stronger and more

determined to live our lives with joy and meaning. Some say, "That which does not kill us only makes us stronger." We will face our adversities and say, "It is not if you can. It is if you will."

The Bikini Team Spring Training Regime reflects this new strength and determination. It is very intense. You will discover the hours add up to more than the usual number. This is of no concern to us. Only mere mortals are bound by the twenty-four-hour day. We goddesses are free of such mundane, temporal limitations.

You are now cordially invited to begin the Bikini Team Spring Training Regime. Let us gently encourage each other to prepare not only for the Season Opener and the work of the summer, but also for The Bikini Team Calendar Photo Shoot.

Always remember, "Bikini is a state of mind."

Yours truly,

Coach Haley

cc: CEO Haley

The Bikini Team Pre-Test

1. Find your uniform. Hint: It is hiding in the back of your lingerie drawer.

2. Put on your uniform.

3. Stand with your back to a full-length mirror.

4. Use a handheld mirror to examine your reflection. **

5. Ask yourself these questions:

   A. Do I look beautiful?

   B. Do I feel beautiful?

   C. Am I bikini-able?

6. Save your answers to compare with your answers on the Post-Test.

Happy Training!

**Pre-Test Warning: Objects seen in the mirror may be as large as they appear.

The Bikini Team Spring Training Regime

Step One: Physical Exercise

Weight Training: 3 sessions per week, 1 hour per session;

Cardio: 4 sessions per week, 1 hour per session;

Abdominal Crunches: 300 per day.

The demands of tanning, especially the contorted positions required of the difficult back work, require that our bodies be in prime physical condition. Therefore, all times, repetitions, and amounts are minimums. Yes, you may do more, but remember our team motto, "No pain, no pain."

Step Two: Sleep

8 hours per night

Rest on scented, freshly ironed linen sheets in a beautiful room filled with flowers.

Step Three: Dining

3 hours per day

Dining should never be rushed. Linger over your meals. Listen to beautiful music as you sip your morning coffee. Share delicious secrets with a teammate as you toy with a gourmet salad at lunch. Graciously accept compliments as you sip champagne before your evening meal. Please remember to limit yourself to reasonable amounts of healthy food and to one delicacy per day. Calories count! This is not the Caftan Team!

Step Four: Readings

2 hours per day

Choose wisely. Fantasies can soothe the soul.

Step Five: Naps

1 hour per day

You may choose to nap alone or with a companion.

Step Six: Massages (received, not given)

2 hours per day

This is the perfect way to awaken from a nap.

Step Seven: Meditation

1 hour per day

Our spirits must be pampered. Release your mind from worrisome thoughts. Mental anguish causes wrinkles.

Step Eight: Entertainment

3 hours per day

Members will freely choose their own forms of amusement. Goddesses are permitted the occasional splurge.

Step Nine: Flirtations

2 hours per day

Flirtations should be at a high level and of an intense nature. This is a great way to burn calories.

Step Ten: Sex

3 hours per day

Member discretion is encouraged, but not required.

All steps of the Spring Training Regime are required each day. We must be in top form if our team is to be successful. The only acceptable excuse for missing a step is that you have found something that is more fun to do. For example: You meet a new friend and you spend the entire day working on Step Ten.

Examples of unacceptable excuses: self-sacrifice, work, or other responsibilities. Time restraints may be lessened by combining steps.

Dining may be combined with Entertainment.

Flirting may be combined with Exercise.

Sex should not be combined with Reading, nor

with Sleep.

Bonus points may be earned for manicures, pedicures, facials, and other forms of self-indulgence.

Team Members who have a significant discrepancy between their ability and their achievement may qualify for an Individual Training Program (ITP). Please see our Exceptional Teammate Coordinator for information on eligibility and testing.

Good luck in your training!

The Bikini Team Post-Test

1. Find your uniform. Hint: It is on the towel rack in the bathroom.

2. Put on your uniform.

3. Stand with your back to a full-length mirror.

4. Using a hand-held mirror, examine your reflection.

5. Ask yourself these questions:

   A. Do I look more beautiful?

   B. Do I feel more beautiful?

   C. Am I a true goddess?

Scoring

Compare your answers to your Pre-Test answers.

Contemplate your success.

Give yourself one point for each Post-Test question answered with a "yes" and zero points for each question answered with a "no."

3 points = Summa Cum Laude

2 points = Magna Cum Laude

1 point = Cum Laude

0 points = Crash and Burn. Quit your job immediately and go on a long cruise. Try again next year.

Remember: No Team Member Left Behind (NTMLB). Or No Behind Left, Child (NBLC).

Congratulations! You have completed The Bikini Team Spring Training Regime!

Team Approved Recipes for Chapter 2

Step 1: Physical Exercise

The best way to start your morning . . .

<u>FRUIT SMOOTHIE</u>

2 cups orange juice

1 frozen banana

1 kiwi, unpeeled

a handful of strawberries

1 fresh peach (use canned in fruit juice in winter)

1/2 box low fat tofu

3 tablespoons flaxseed

Place all ingredients in a blender and whir away. Of course you can mix and match other fruits. We like the frozen blueberries and the canned pineapple, too.

Step 2: Sleep

The land of nod . . .

<u>KEY LIME PIE MARTINIS</u>

4 parts Stolichnaya vanilla vodka

1 part Key lime juice

1 part sugar syrup (recipe follows)

1 part pineapple juice

Simple Syrup

Boil 1 part sugar to 1 part water for 5 minutes. Keep in fridge. Mix all ingredients in a cocktail shaker with ice. Pour into frosty martini glasses. Sip, then sleep.

Step 3: Dining

Sometimes you want something special, some calories, some alcohol, some chocolate . . .

MESCLUN SALAD WITH WHITE WINE VINAIGRETTE

fresh mesclun greens

pear slices

blue cheese crumbles

roasted pecans

slivered red onion

white wine vinaigrette (recipe follows)

Prepare salad and place on individual salad plates. Prepare dressing and serve alongside salad.

White Wine Vinaigrette

1 cup canola oil

1/4 cup white wine vinegar

1/4 cup balsamic vinegar

scant 1/2 cup sugar

4 teaspoons salt

1 teaspoon freshly ground pepper

Mix all ingredients in an attractive bottle. Shake well until sugar is dissolved. Keeps in fridge for days.

PASTA WITH VODKA CREAM SAUCE

1 tablespoon extra-virgin olive oil

1 tablespoon butter

2 cloves garlic, minced

2 shallots, minced

1 cup vodka

1 cup chicken stock

1 32-ounce can crushed tomatoes

coarse salt and freshly ground pepper

16 ounces penne rigate

1/2 cup heavy cream

20 leaves fresh basil, shredded or torn

crusty bread and a dish of olive oil for dipping

Heat a large skillet over moderate heat. Add oil, butter, garlic, and shallots. Gently sauté shallots for 3 to 5 minutes to develop their sweetness. Add vodka to the pan. Reduce vodka by half: this will take 2 or 3 minutes. Add chicken stock and tomatoes. Bring sauce to a bubble and reduce heat to simmer. Season with salt and pepper. While sauce simmers, cook pasta in salted boiling water. Stir cream into sauce. When sauce returns to a bubble, remove from heat. Drain pasta. Toss hot pasta with sauce and basil leaves. Pass pasta with crusty bread and extra virgin olive oil for dipping.

CHOCOLATE POTS DE CREME

2/3 cup whole milk

1 egg

2 tablespoons sugar

pinch salt

1 cup semi-sweet chocolate chips

2 tablespoons hazelnut liqueur

1 cup whipping cream

2 tablespoons sugar

Heat milk in a small pan over medium heat until it just comes to a boil. In a blender, combine egg, sugar, a pinch of salt, chocolate chips, and liqueur. Turn on blender to low setting. Pour in boiling milk in a slow stream. Blend 1 minute, until smooth. Spoon chocolate into 4 custard cups and chill. When ready to serve, beat cream until soft peaks form. Add a little sugar and beat to combine. Top the chocolate cups with a dollop of whipped cream.

Step 4: Reading

Curl up on the sofa with a good book and enjoy . . .

<u>SOY CHAI TEA LATTE</u>

2 chai tea bags

1 cup boiling water

Steep for 5 minutes in a large (at least 2-cup capacity) mug.

Soy Mixture

1 cup vanilla soy milk

Microwave until just boiling. Add

1 tablespoon sugar

When tea has steeped, remove teabag. Pour soy mixture into a large jar with a lid or a vacuum-sealed travel cup. Stand over the sink and shake vigorously to create foam. Carefully and slowly remove top and pour foamy soy mixture into mug. Do not stir.

Step 5-7: Nap, massages, meditation

We don't eat while sleeping, meditating, or getting a massage . . .

Step 8: Entertainment

Good food, good friends, good music, and alcohol spell entertainment . . .

<u>TEQUILA LIME CHICKEN</u>

1/2 cup gold tequila

1 cup freshly squeezed lime juice (5 to 6 limes)

1/2 cup freshly squeezed orange juice (2 oranges)

1 tablespoon chili powder

1 tablespoon minced fresh jalapeno pepper (1 pepper seeded)

1 tablespoon minced fresh garlic (3 cloves)

2 teaspoons kosher salt

1 teaspoon freshly ground black pepper

3 whole (6 split) boneless chicken breasts, skin on

Combine the tequila, lime juice, orange juice, chili powder, jalapeno pepper, garlic, salt, and pepper in a large bowl. Add the chicken breasts. Refrigerate overnight. Heat the grill. Remove the chicken breasts from the marinade, sprinkle well with salt and pepper, and grill them skin-side down for about 5 minutes, until nicely browned. Turn the chicken and cook for another 10 minutes, until just cooked through. Remove from the grill to a plate. Cover tightly and allow to rest for 5 minutes. Serve hot or at room temperature.

Step 9: Flirtation

A coquettish cocktail . . .

<u>COSMOPOLITANS</u>

4 parts Absolut Citron

2 parts cranberry juice

2 parts triple sec

1 part lime juice

splash sweet and sour mix

Mix in a cocktail shaker with ice and pour into frosty martini glasses. Flirt away.

Step 10: Sex

Sometimes all you have time for is a . . .

.

QUICK ROLL

-
1 package refrigerator biscuits

3/4 cup orange marmalade or apricot or peach all fruit
jam

melted butter

Spread marmalade or jam in bottom of a 9" cake pan
that has been *well* greased. Take biscuits and separate
them and roll in melted butter. Put the biscuits in the
pan and bake at 400° for 20 minutes. Remove from
oven and let stand 3 minutes before turning over on a
serving plate.

And sometimes you end up with . . .

STICKY BUNS

24 frozen rolls

Layer frozen rolls in buttered bundt pan.

Mix and sprinkle over rolls:
3/4 cup brown sugar

1 small box vanilla pudding (do NOT use instant)

3/4 cup pecans

Melt 1 stick of butter and pour over mixture. Put into oven overnight (uncovered) to let rise. In the morning, take pan out of the oven and preheat oven to 350 degrees. Bake for 20 to 30 minutes. When done, let set in pan for 15 minutes. Invert on a large plate. Make sure your plate is considerably larger than the bundt pan.

And sometimes you just want to . . .

<u>KOODLE THE NOODLE</u>

1 cup low fat milk

1 cup vanilla yogurt

1 cup low fat cottage cheese

3 eggs

1 teaspoon cinnamon

1/2 cup sugar

1 box (8-ounce) medium wide egg noodles, cooked
and drained

1 cup golden raisins

2 tablespoons sugar, mixed with 1 teaspoon cinnamon

2 teaspoons butter

Heat oven to 350 degrees. Butter a 9-inch square baking
dish and set aside. In a blender, combine milk, yogurt,
cottage cheese, eggs, cinnamon, and sugar until smooth.
Pour mixture into a large bowl. Combine with noodles
and raisins. Place mixture in a baking dish. Sprinkle
with cinnamon-sugar mixture and dot with butter. Bake
50-60 minutes or until pudding is golden brown. Serve
warm or at room temperature.

Chapter 3:
Bikini ABCs

A B C. Simple as one two three. A B C. One two three.
Do re mi. . . . You get the idea.

A – **Abs**: they don't have to be six-packs to be
presentable. Tan abs look tighter!

B – **Bikini** (of course): if you're going to splurge,
this is the place to do it. Individual taste reigns.

C – **Costumes**: wear costumes instead of dressing
for success. Red boots, rhinestone sandals,
boas—they all make a statement.

D – **Dress-up**: when you have to dress up in the summer, you can wear your bikini underneath. We've had them on under dresses at graduation and during business meetings. One team member wore hers underneath her suit during an NPR interview so as not to waste time getting straight to the pool.

E – **Energy and Estrogen**: they are co-dependents.

F – **Friendship, floats, fun, flip flops**

G – **Goddesses,** including our daughters, goddesses in training: Abby, Beth, and Lacy; **also grooming:** visible hair is a turn-off. Cynthia says, "Use any removal means necessary, from scissors to a chain saw."

H – **Hair color**: in one way or another, we're all chemically dependent.

I – **Igloo**: not a good location for Bikini Team meetings.

J – **Juggle**: set priorities to make every Bikini Team meeting you possibly can.

K – **Kisses** (love 'em); **Kudos** (please, may we have some more?); **Knee-jerk** (not our style); **Karaoke** (proceed with caution); **Kit™, Bikini-Adaptor** (a life-saver).

L – **Love** yourself, your family, your friends, and your team.

M – **Myopia, Menopause, Manicures, Massages, Mylanta**: not necessarily in that order.

N – **Nothing (birthday suit)**: dress code for sleeping, skinny dipping, deserted beaches.

O – **Oprah**: we're on our way!

P – **Politics**: Bikini is a radical political statement, but avoid much political discussion at team meetings.

Q – **Quit**: although we'd love to quit our pesky day jobs, we still feel like **Queens**.

R – **Ratchet** up the party atmosphere, but **Relax** by the pool.

S – **Shopping**: Lina and Nancy hate it; Ann finds bargains in nearby consignment shops; Cynthia avidly orders from catalogs.

T – **Throw** away all underwear that doesn't make you feel like a goddess.

U – **Uterus**: once you've finished with it, throw it away, too.

V – **Vogue**: describes Bikini Team philosophies, especially not taking yourself too seriously.

W – **Wear** a smile: it's free, eye-catching, and contagious.

X – **X-out** the unimportant stuff in your life. Save time for the most important—playing with your teammates.

Y (MCA) – a favorite Bikini Team hangout.

Z – **Zen**: 1) the essence of tanning; 2) state obtained while tanning.

Goddess-worthy, A-B-C Recipes for Chapter 3

Goddesses: when we're good, we're very good . . .

<u>*ANGEL*</u> FOOD CAKE

1 1/2 cups sifted cake flour

12 large egg whites

1/2 teaspoon salt

1 1/2 teaspoons cream of tartar

1 3/4 cups sifted granulated sugar

1 1/2 teaspoons pure vanilla extract

1/2 teaspoon pure almond extract

Preheat oven to 275 degrees with rack in center. Sift flour four times. In the bowl of an electric mixer, beat egg whites and salt until foamy. Add cream of tartar, and continue beating until soft peaks form. With machine running, add sugar in a slow, steady stream, beating until fully incorporated and stiff glossy peaks form. Add vanilla and almond extracts, and beat to combine. Remove from mixer. Gradually add flour, gently but thoroughly, folding it into egg-white mixture until fully combined. Pour into an ungreased angel-food-cake pan. Cut through batter with a knife to remove air bubbles. Bake 30 minutes. Increase temperature to 325 degrees and bake 30 minutes more. Cool, inverted, 1 hour before removing from pan.

All goddesses deserve champagne and caviar . . .

BODACIOUS EMPRESS CAVIAR

3 hard-cooked eggs

salt, pepper and mayonnaise to taste

1 / 2 cup sour cream

3- to 4-ounce jar caviar, either red or black

chopped green onion

Mash eggs with salt, pepper, and mayonnaise and put into a small bowl. Chill. Unmold onto a serving dish and cover with sour cream. Top with caviar and green onion. Refrigerate until serving.

. . . and chocolate!

<u>*CHOCOLATE* DIPPED STRAWBERRIES</u>

1/2 cup semisweet chocolate chips

6 tablespoons heavy cream

12 long-stemmed strawberries

Melt the chocolate and cream together in a bowl set over simmering water until just melted. Stir and remove from the heat. Dip each strawberry in the chocolate and set aside on waxed or parchment paper to dry. Must serve with champagne.

Chapter 4:
Imaginary Friends

Those of us who know, admire, and love the Serene Miss Haley have long wondered how she manages to stay so . . . serene. In this brief chapter, Miss Haley discloses one—and perhaps the most important—of her secrets: her relationships with her imaginary friends . . .

Imaginary friends can become your virtual best friends. They require very little, they never leave a mess, and their gossip is delicious. Allow me to introduce you to three of my imaginary friends.

Rita Rene Wortman-Wooten

Rita Rene is a former imaginary friend, but I hold out hope of hearing back from her one day.

I first met Rita Rene some years ago on the bridal page of our local newspaper. There amidst all the angelic faces of sweet, young brides, was a young woman who looked suspiciously like Dolly Parton. Or, to be more precise, she looked like a young man impersonating Dolly Parton. The bouffant hair and heavy make-up accented her masculine, chiseled face, giving away her secret. She was a drag queen pretending to be a bride. Oh, horrors!

I quickly cut out her picture and took it to our Sunday afternoon Bikini Team meeting. The teammates were enchanted. We had never seen a wedding dress cut so low, make-up so heavy, hair so big! It was love at first sight!

Soon after, Rita Rene started writing to us. She would send us e-mails. She would deliver handwritten letters to our mailboxes. She wanted to join The Team.

We sent her a copy of our book, *How to Score High on the Bikini Team Admissions Test*, and one of our application folders. We don't know if it was the length of the application, the three required essays, or the $500.00 non-refundable application fee that scared her off, but we never heard from her again.

Dear Bikini Team Members,
    I want you all to know how deeply hurt I am that once again I was not invited to your mountain retreat weekend! Also, I was deeply hurt that I did not win a trophy! Willie Van my loving husband, said I should have won "Most Sexiest" and I agree! W.V. also says I shouldn't worry about this but I am just so deeply hurt! I just hope and pray that one day y'all will invite me to be a real member of your team! Until that day I will always be deeply hurt!   XXX OOO, Peace and Love,
                                        Rita Rene ♡

This was when we amended our Membership Policy to read as follows: "The Bikini Team will take no new members."

Years passed. Our hearts softened. We decided if we were going to help humankind, we needed to take

61

in new members. Our new Membership Policy reads, "We will save the world, one woman at a time." That means you, too, Rita Rene.

Boots

Boots is the lady who takes care of my house. She comes approximately once a week, or whenever she likes. She wears red cowboy boots and sings and dances as she magically restores order to my life. She loves cleaning. She loves her job. She loves life.

Boots is not judgmental. She never asks, "Why is she so messy?" "Why doesn't she put her shoes away?" "Does she have to get out a new glass every time she has a drink of water?" "Why doesn't she ever hang up those wet bikinis and towels?" She simply cooks, cleans, organizes, and tenderly massages the house. She even makes minor repairs.

Boots is good at her job. She takes pride in her work. She has attainable goals. She provides a valuable service. She helps people. She simplifies my life.

Zack

Zack is my imaginary gardener. He loves to mow the grass. He can spend eight hours on a lawn mower and then go for the weed eater. Planting trees and spraying Round Up are his passions. He is happiest cleaning the yard after a big storm. Hurricane Hugo was his dream come true.

He loves flowers. He knows what to plant and when to plant it. He studies the schedule of the blooms throughout the seasons and uses that information to determine the color scheme of the garden. He understands the complex nature of roses. We travel the world together, visiting the great formal gardens, examining the wildflowers, and collecting ideas to recreate at home. He is a true botanical artist.

His vegetable gardens are legendary. He creates his own recipes and cooks our healthy dinners using only his homegrown organic herbs and vegetables. His gazpacho is the best in the world.

What's more, he loves to fix things. The sight of a burned-out light bulb makes him run for the ladder. He fixes garbage disposals, water pumps, computers, and televisions. The lawn mower blade is sharpened regularly.

The sun glistening on his muscled back as he toils is a beautiful sight. At dusk we go for long promenades along the walking path he has built for me. He writes beautiful poetry and reads it aloud to me as we sit beside the creek.

Ah, Zack, where are you?

Other Bikini Team members do not indulge in relationships with imaginary friends. This is why Miss Haley would be especially pleased for her friends to hear from anyone in our reading audience about their friends. You can write her friends at <u>Boots@hotmaids. com</u>, <u>Zach@hotmale.com</u>, <u>Rita-Rene@supportgroup. com</u>.

Recipes for Chapter 4
Imaginary recipes . . . drink enough of these and you can have imaginary friends too!

<u>MARGARITA – RENE'S</u>

1 part good tequila

1 part triple sec

1 part fresh lime juice

1 part simple syrup (recipe follows)

splash club soda

Mix above in a shaker with ice. Shake and pour into salt rimmed glasses. Turn on some salsa music, and dance the night away!

Simple Syrup

1 part water to 2 parts sugar. Boil until sugar is dissolved and keep in fridge.

BOOTS' ORGASMIC CHOCOLATE

4 tablespoons butter

4 marshmallows

8 tablespoons chocolate chips

Melt all 3 ingredients over slow heat. Pour over ice cream. The sauce hardens upon contact.

ZACK'S GAZPACHO

8 large, fresh tomatoes, quartered

3 to 4 cloves of garlic, peeled

2 large cucumbers, chunked

1 large pepper, cored, seeded and quartered

a few radishes

1 hot banana pepper, seeded

small bunch arugula

2 ribs celery, chunked

1/2 medium onion, chunked

parsley leaves

splash extra virgin olive oil

tarragon vinegar

salt and freshly ground pepper to taste

sugar to taste

Process tomatoes and garlic in food processor in batches until fairly smooth. At the end of processing each batch, add some of the veggies and pulse. Pour each batch into a large bowl. Do not allow the mixture to purée (keep it chunky). Continue until all veggies and herbs are processed. Season mixture with oil, vinegar, salt, pepper, and sugar. Keeps in fridge for at least a week.

Chapter 4 ½:
Our Physical Trainer,
Madame Jill LaLanne

(When we suggested to Coach Haley that Jill be a part of Chapter 4, she told us in no uncertain terms that Jill didn't fit in Chapter 4 because Jill isn't imaginary and that, moreover, Jill wanted her own chapter. One proof that Jill is real, says Coach Haley, is that she has her own e-mail account. This half-chapter is all Jill's.)

Physical training must include change in order to be successful. Coach Haley knew that even the highly effective Bikini Team Spring Training Regime needed a little something different after the first few years of guiding the Teammates. So she hired a physical trainer, Madame Jill LaLanne, a 155-year-old French clairvoyant, who began observing the Teammates through astral projection and psychically e-training them. Jill's first review of the Team arrived on a cold January morning.

Imagine the surprise of the Teammates as they read Jill's first e-mail on their office computers . . .

Dear Members of the Bikini Team,

Allow me to introduce myself. I am Madame Jill LaLanne. I am a Certified Clairvoyant Psychic Physical Trainer and I am here to help you to get into the best shape of your life.

First of all, I would like to thank Coach Haley and to say how happy I am that she has hired me to work with the members of the Bikini Team. I have studied and analyzed your Bikini Team Spring Training Regime and have found it to be a remarkable program. Follow it precisely, faithfully, and religiously and you will be transformed into goddesses by your Season Opener, at the end of May.

I plan to monitor you through my extrasensory perception and my astral projections, offering advice as needed. During my first week of observations, I have seen that all of you are working very hard. I have also noticed some areas that need improvement. Please accept the following suggestions:

Ann – A half gallon of ice cream does not equal one Daily Delicacy. Be careful. Calories count.

Nancy – You are not getting the required amount of sleep. And let's get a man in that bed.

Cary – Drink up and party more. You are not consuming enough alcohol.

Cynthia – You are spending too much time with scholarly readings. Shakespeare may be intellectually stimulating, but he is still dead. Dead men have their physical limitations.

Lina – You are spending entirely too much time on housework. Try meditating more often using this mantra, "Dust, you are my friend."

None of you are spending the required amount of time on sex. Let's concentrate on getting our priorities in order. I know that together we can make great progress.

Only eighteen weeks to go! Let's get to work!

Sincerely,

Jill

Madame Jill LaLanne, CCPPT, SAP

Certified Clairvoyant Psychic Physical Trainer

Specialist in Astral Projection

Jill's e-mails arrived each month. In February she wrote . . .

Dear Members of the Bikini Team,

The snow and ice of the past few days have given you a brief respite from your usual hectic schedules. I requested this storm so that you could begin learning to read the signs of nature.

A snow day is a sign that you need to relax and pamper yourself. Sleep as late as you like, play, sit by the fire, drink red wine, snuggle. Under no circumstances should you waste this precious day cleaning out your closets or doing work for "S."

As I sit here in my studio on Parc Monceau in Paris, I meditate on your training and your questions come to me. Allow me to share some answers with you.

Ann, yes, your career as an e-mailist and cyber-coach will be very profitable.

Cary, yes, the weather will be perfect on your daughter's wedding day.

Cynthia, no, no, no, no, no! Not only are your ideas dangerous to yourself and others, they would scandalize your entire community!

Lina, no, the Dallas Cowboys will not make a comeback next year.

Nancy, yes, you should start dating.

There is no need to thank me. This service is part of my work as your clairvoyant psychic physical trainer. Remember, we have only fourteen weeks!

Sincerely,

Jill

Madame Jill LaLanne, CCPPT, SAP

Certified Clairvoyant Psychic Physical Trainer

Specialist in Astral Projection

March brought some personal news about Jill . . .

Dear Members of the Bikini Team,

Tomorrow is the first day of spring, and also my birthday. As you may recall, I was born on March 20, 1850, in Paris. Please do not feel that you must shower me with gifts or even attention.

I would prefer instead that you use this day to begin the more serious portion of your Spring Training Regime. You have only nine weeks until your Season Opener. I sense that some of you are not ready to don the uniform of your Team. I see that there is serious work to do. Please do your best.

Fondly,

Jill

Madame Jill LaLanne, CCPPT, SAP

Certified Clairvoyant Psychic Physical Trainer

Specialist in Astral Projection

Some of the Teammates responded to Jill's birthday, and bonding began to take place. Some would send Jill questions or express their own opinions about issues. Jill always tried to encourage every member. In April she wrote . . .

Dearest Members of the Bikini Team,

Thank you all very much for the kind letters and beautiful cards you sent for my birthday. Ann, the flowers were beautiful! You are all, truly, my favorite pupils.

Cary, I flew over your house yesterday and was awed by your amazing azaleas. I see that your training is going very well. Your abdominals are phenomenal. You will be in top shape for the Season Opener!

I see that Cynthia has been working diligently at the gym, Nancy is working on creating a timesaving and safe way to tan, while Ann is working on napping and eating delicacies. Brava Ladies!

Lina, you must relax or you will explode. Running does not count if you are thinking about work while you are running. You must learn to run and smile at the same time.

Please keep in mind, it is only five weeks until the Season Opener!

With warmest regards,

Jill

Madame Jill LaLanne, CCPPT, SAP

Certified Clairvoyant Psychic Physical Trainer

Specialist in Astral Projection

At the end of May, the day before the Season Opener, Ann wrote a frantic e-mail to Jill . . .

Dear Jill,

As you know, the Season Opener is tomorrow. I am going to meet all my Teammates at the pool and my belly is going to scare the living daylights out of them. Could you give me some advice on how I can lose ten pounds in twenty-four hours? I know this might be a bit difficult, but you are such a special trainer. If anyone can save me, it is you!

Thanks so much,

Ann

Jill was irritated and responded to Ann's request with ridicule . . .

Dear Ann,

Never fear, your extra ten pounds can easily be gone by tomorrow. All you have to do is cut off one of your arms. That should teach you to be more diligent in your Spring Training.

By the way, all of your Teammates have been successful in their training. They all look beautiful and fit.

Jill

Madame Jill LaLanne, CCPPT, SAP

Certified Clairvoyant Psychic Physical Trainer

Specialist in Astral Projection

Ann worked extra hard to get back in shape quickly, and Jill eventually forgave her for her temporary lack of focus on training. In June Jill decided it was time for a little positive reinforcement . . .

My Dear Members of the Bikini Team,

Congratulations! You have successfully completed your Spring Training Regime and you are in top form. Your Post-Tests show that you all look beautiful, feel beautiful, and are true goddesses. I have a gift for you to thank you for your hard work.

I have decided to give you the gift of your most beloved memory. This is a memory which will often come to you in your later years as you sit in quiet reflection, a memory of an event which has not yet happened. I give you this gift of a future memory so that you may enjoy it now and for many years to come. These memories will comfort you in your final moments.

Cynthia, you have a memory of great wealth. You are seeing yourself ten years from now, looking back to the summer of 2005. You see that the publishing of <u>Bikini Is a State of Mind</u> was a turning point in your career. You laugh and tell your new lover, "I am paid more in royalties in one day now than I was paid for one year of teaching at Davidson College."

Cary, you have a memory of your granddaughter's wedding day. Little Cary is worried about the weather and all the details of the ceremony. She wants everything to be perfect. You calm her by telling her, once again, her favorite story since childhood, the story of that magical day, the beautiful island wedding of her mother and father, way back in October 2004.

Ann, your memory is of the day your new school finally opened. When you won the 2006 $900 million South Carolina Powerball Lottery, you knew exactly what to do with the money. You wrote the curriculum, financed, designed, and built a school where whole families live and attend classes together, and where they are taught how to escape from illiteracy and poverty. Your innovative ideas dramatically changed public education, saved millions of lives, and won you a Nobel Prize.

Nancy, you have a memory of applause and laughter. You are a very old lady looking back at your wonderful, happy life thinking, "How right I was to return to the stage! My twenty years of teaching were important, but acting was my first and true love." Your Academy Awards were all well deserved.

Lina, you too have a memory of yourself as an older woman. You are thinking back to the time you first saw the life partner of your later years. He looked so strong and handsome in that Dallas Cowboys uniform. It was love at first sight, but it was many years before you admitted it. And now you have been living together for twenty years. Your children are grown. You have your Ph.D. You have retired from your endowed professorship at Rice University. You have never been happier than you are now living with the distinguished Senator from the Great State of Texas, the Honorable Emmit Smith.

Enjoy your memories now, dear ladies, now and in your future.

With great affection, I remain
your faithful trainer,
Jill
Madame Jill LaLanne, CCPPT, SAP
Certified Clairvoyant Psychic Physical Trainer
Specialist in Astral Projection

Coach Haley and her Teammates were all so grateful to Jill for her generous gift of their favorite future memories that they decided to renew Jill's contract to e-train the Bikini Team for the next 155 years.

Recipe for Chapter 4 ½

<u>MADAME JILL LALANNE'S KIR ROYALE</u>

1 chilled bottle of a good French champagne

3 teaspoons crème de cassis liqueur

Pour 1 teaspoon of Crème de Cassis into each of 6 champagne glasses. Fill each glass with champagne. Enjoy immediately!

Chapter 5:
A Brief History
of the Bikini

A history of the bikini should be brief. Besides, brevity is the soul of wit.

If you have ever seen Raquel Welsh in the movie *One Million Years B.C.*, you might say the bikini rightfully dates back to the Stone Age. But more academic research reveals the first documented bikini wearers on a mosaic in the Piazza Armerina in Sicily between 200-300 A.D. (We don't think the mosaic was there for only one hundred years, but the date of the mosaic's origin is a little sketchy.) This first Bikini Team display features eight women (rather than our total of five) *sporting* (of course) bikinis.

This must have been an awesome team because there is no other evidence of the sport until the 1930s. The team either disappeared or was too controversial to be discussed in public. But in the thirties, five inches of a woman's midriff were liberated when the two-piece bathing suit became acceptable. Although the navel remained under cover, the abs were exposed. The bikini had nearly arrived.

In the 1940s, the bikini made an "explosive" debut, but for the next decade, it was essentially banished to the pages of dirty men's magazines (that would be dirty magazines, not dirty men). The birth of the bikini began in 1943 with the wartime rationing of fabric used in women's swimwear. On July 1, 1946, the United States tested the first nuclear weapon on several small islands in the Pacific, known as the Bikini Atoll. News of the atomic bomb covered the papers and quickly became the talk of every town, even Davidson, North Carolina.

Frenchman Louis Réard seized on the opportunity to design and market a new style, and, four days after the test, on July 5, 1946, the bikini was born. Réard named his suit the "bikini"—explosive because so dangerously compact. He revealed his masterpiece at a poolside fashion show in Paris.

The suit was modeled by Micheline Bernardini, a woman with no qualms about showing skin. Micheline was not a teacher, like the members of our Bikini Team. She worked as a stripper. Consisting of a mere thirty inches of fabric (remember the war rations), four triangles and a few pieces of string, the first bikini was sold in what appeared to be a matchbox. (Around the same time, Frenchman Jacques Heim introduced his two-piece commemoration of nuclear testing, called the "Atome," but it was not nearly as revealing as the bikini.)

You won't believe what happened on the day after Réard's announcement (July 6, 1946). Nothing. The invention of the bikini was received in total silence.

By 1948, Catholics must have gotten wind of this invention, however, because they banned bikinis in several countries, including Spain, Portugal, and Italy. While bikinis were never officially banned in America, few women, except Big Lina, dared to wear them for the first fifteen years after their invention. And, for many years, decency leagues pressured Hollywood to keep them off the screen.

But in the fifties, things began to rock and roll. That's when hips became hip, so women could expose them a bit more. At the beginning of the decade, the strapless bathing suit emerged, so women could at least fully expose their shoulders and avoid those horrible tan lines. Bikinis were worn, but still considered shamefully indecent by the general public. After the 1951 Miss World Contest, bikinis were officially banned from all beauty contests. According to *Elle* magazine, they were deemed an "Unfair advantage to the wearer and potentially dangerous to the health of some judges." Soon movie stars jumped in to rescue the bikini. Bridget Bardot, Anna Ekberg, and Sophia Loren made their way across the silver screen in bikinis, and the public responded by wearing 3D glasses in theaters.

Spandex brought a new cling to skimpy swimwear at the end of the decade.

Years after its acceptance in France, Italy, Brazil, and Spain (even by the Catholics), the bikini finally made its debut on modest America's beaches in the early 1960s. Hollywood, pop music, and *Sports Illustrated* (see? sports again) influenced the growth and acceptance of the bikini as a viable and desirable swimsuit option. Ursula Andress, Annette Funicello (from *The Mickey Mouse Club*), Raquel Welsh, and Jane Fonda graced the movie screens while Brian Hyland sang of the "Itsy-Bitsy Teenie-Weenie Yellow Polka-Dot Bikini." Babette March, outfitted in a bikini, was on the cover of the first swimsuit issue of *Sports Illustrated*. During this decade, over 100 beach movies were produced. For the first time, youth, rock 'n' roll, and the bikini-clad body reigned supreme.

During the 1970s, less was acknowledged as better. The erogenous zones migrated from the breasts and midriff to the upper thighs. The string bikini (less fabric, more thighs) and the thong (think Japanese Sumo wrestlers) were introduced. The thong didn't catch on as well. Perhaps that is because it was commonly known as "dental floss," and some consumers had a hard time finding the thong in the local drug store.

Health concerns about the dangers of sun exposure affected bikini sales during the 1980s. Apparently some women thought the sun damage would be lessened if they covered their tummies because bikini sales constituted only about one-third of the women's bathing suit market. Réard's company folded in 1988.

With the 1990s, and the genesis of the Bikini Team, the bikini became a staple part of American swimwear. The ideal body was toned and rigorously conditioned, but even those less than ideal bodies could do justice to the bikini. Bikini became a state of mind. When the bikini debuted, many questioned whether it could or would stay on, but now it is clear: the bikini is here to stay.

Chapter 6:
Our Nemesis

Living with opposites prepares us for life's challenges. Summer has winter, yen has yang, and the Bikini Goddess has PITA. Merely hearing the word PITA sends shivers down our spines, for a PITA is the very essence of a woman we avoid. A PITA is our nemesis.

PITA defined: PAIN IN THE ASS.

PITA Characteristics

To better understand the PITA, think of someone you know who is infatuated with herself. You may think of several women. Let us explore further. Focus on a woman who is not only self-centered, but so self-absorbed that she has no meaningful relationships with other women. You may also focus on a woman who is demanding and downright devious.

To the Bikini Goddess, PITAs are self-indulgent women engrossed in their own activities. They believe that other women are of little value. When a PITA asks how your day is going, be aware that the question is superficial, for a PITA thinks only of herself. In fact, the PITA woman concentrates on such questions as, "Do you think I'm clever?" and "Am I pretty today?" The PITA is self-infatuated; she is the female narcissist!

On the other hand, the Bikini Goddess puts others' needs before her own. She enjoys life. We all energetically work to strengthen our friends and colleagues, and we welcome new associations. As proactive women, we bring honor to our many roles as women, mothers, and leaders in our careers. If we demand, we demand of ourselves. We set a high bar. Thus, in the final analysis, the PITA image is the antithesis of our persona; the PITA woman is our direct opposite.

The PITA Principle

The PITA Principle is a clear concept. One underlying code is that to be the very best PITA, one must be a whiner. PITAs have perfected their whining to such a science that, if moaning and whimpering do not produce the desired outcomes, they resort to all-out pouting until they get their way. The PITA has no shame!

The PITA Principle sets up a negative standard for women—that women must rely on feeble ploys to gain their desires. PITAs are fixed in time and have not shifted to the paradigm that women can attain their objectives on their own.

Bikini Goddesses never stoop to such shenanigans. Empowered with knowledge and self-respect, we set our sights and accomplish our chosen objectives. We truly believe the old cliché that if there is a will, there is a way. Bikini women aim high and make it happen.

We simply Power-Down to get the job done. Whining would never enter our minds, for it is beneath us. We believe that sulking is a waste of energy and that, because we are goddesses, we *rise* above the constant droning from a PITA.

PITA and the Team Concept

Sadly, the word *Team* is not part of PITA's vocabulary. PITAs are not team players because they are very much about what others can do for them. The troubling fact is that the PITA does not know her own identity. She finds it difficult to understand and accept women. The PITA believes she is above her women friends and often creates fictional stories to boost her self-worth. This loftiness sets her apart and does not serve her well in forming close bonds.

A PITA's poor understanding of a team is most evident when a group gathers for events and even more pronounced during travel. While on retreats with your girl friends, have you ever noticed that one in your group is never around when it is time for domestic responsibilities? You may have a PITA among you. Be prepared for the PITA woman to allow you to wait on her. She will also be the one who arrives without her assigned items because she was too busy entertaining herself before the trip to collect them. The PITA would never plan ahead of time, anticipating what other members of her group would enjoy, because the group concept is not part of her world. A PITA would most likely wonder, and even expect, that other members in the entourage have shopped with her in mind. Don't plan to have an interactive group discussion, in which all members contribute to the dialogue, because the PITA will expect you to listen and center your conversation on her. The PITA is so demanding of your time that you should consider packing CO_2 bottles for your weekend retreat because she can suck all the positive energy from the room. It is probably best to leave the PITA behind when planning a fun-packed weekend retreat!

In contrast, the word *Team* in our title is the binding force for all Bikini Goddesses. It is the very cement of our group and the motivating passion that invites us to renew our friendship and celebrate our Bikini identity. Each Bikini Goddess understands the Team is her source of strength, support, and absolute enjoyment of camaraderie, for it is the group from which we draw our power. We value the diversity among our group and welcome differing attitudes and opinions. Our Bikini Team openly supports and fosters respect for our individual differences, for we realize that validation of each member's uniqueness provides the creativity and the stimulation to function as a whole. In truth, the sum of all our parts makes our Team.

Are Bikini Women PITA-able?

As goddesses, we know we must maintain our positions. We continually perform self-assessments. We view our responsibilities seriously, and each of us endeavors to be voted *Most Valuable Player* on the Team. We work earnestly to amend silly flaws. Along with our many tasks, striving to be a goddess is a vital part of our daily life. But as goddesses with human bodies, hearts, and minds, we each have moments when we fall victim to a PITA episode. Yes, in truth, we can be "PITA-able"; we can each resemble a PITA. It takes only a quick reminder from a teammate that one of us is having a PITA moment, and without hesitation, that particular individual can snap back into her normal goddess state.

As teammates and good friends, we all know one another's PITA vulnerabilities. Ann, the Bikini Team CEO, is a native South Carolinian. Her geographic origins constantly cause her to move more slowly than the rest of us. The slower-paced South Carolinian has not yet learned that time in North Carolina, home of the Bikini Team, is faster, because we are above South Carolina on the map. Some members of the Bikini Team believe it is time to develop an ITP (Individual Training Plan) to give her the special instruction she needs for being time-challenged. Ann seems to float through time, and to those of us who run on a schedule, her lateness is her PITA tendency.

Nancy is better known as Chatty Cathy. We truly believe that someone pulled her cord, and it will not recoil. Some days we would very much like to cut the cord or wrap it around her neck! Nancy is doll-sized in stature, and we are amazed that such a small person can have such strong, oversized vocal cords. When Nancy has a PITA moment, the team gives her a time-out so that she can rest her voice. If the time-out fails, we have also developed a behavior modification plan that uses positive rewards for controlled talking.

Cary is a bartender's worst nightmare. The fact that Cary likes Corona is not surprising; however, the fact that the lime must be cut exactly to the proportions she requires is too PITA! Cary expects the lime to be precisely the width needed to squeeze through the bottle's neck so that no precious lime juice is lost. We are fearful that one day she may go behind the bar and show the waiter how to cut a perfect lime. Cary is also menu-challenged. She quizzes the waiter at length on all ingredients used in each entrée. This PITA tendency took roots when Cary owned a restaurant and learned how to adapt recipes for various menus. For those of us on the team who are extremely hungry when we are in a restaurant, Cary's deliberation over entrée selections can be taxing. To improve this PITA tendency, we suggest that Cary abstain from restaurants and bars for one whole year.

Cynthia's PITA tendency begins the moment she sets foot in a karaoke establishment. Her disdain for Elton John wannabes precipitates a noticeable physical change. She becomes rigid with her arms crossed tightly, as her body assumes a judgmental pose. As a singer and a member of the *Righteous Sisters,* a lip-synching girl group, she has developed a critical ear for entertainers. Yet Cynthia goes further and becomes Simon on *American Idol.* Sometimes, when she gets downright obstinate, it is best to move to a new location for our Bikini Team's night out. To help her with her PITA moments, the Team feels that one night in Las Vegas with Celine Dion, her least favorite entertainer, will provide Cynthia a new perspective on musical performers.

Lina, who coined the word PITA, is our most high-strung member, and as a result, her "PITA-abilities" surface whenever she is faced with a true PAIN IN THE ASS. Unfortunately, this happens frequently on a daily basis. Her impatience with the PITAs in the world is so prodigious that she would just as soon throw one over the balcony than deal with her. It is an idea she has explored more than once. The PITA gives Lina such a fit that she too becomes crabby, difficult, and overheated. In fact, her skin begins to resemble that of a cooked lobster! The team members are concerned. The goddesses believe the only possible solution is to place Lina with a PITA near a balcony. The targeted outcome is for her to learn patience and sympathy for all PITAs.

Recipes for Chapter 6

Pita pertinent . . . when that crabby PITA annoys you . . .

<u>**CRAB DIP**</u>

1 8-ounce package cream cheese, softened

a blob of mayonnaise

2 or 3 green onions, chopped, or to taste

3 cloves garlic, minced, or to taste

1/2 pound crabmeat

1 can artichoke hearts

Cream the cream cheese and mayo well. Mix in the green onions and garlic. Mix well, then stir in the crab and artichokes. Pour into greased pyrex and bake until bubbly. Serve with crackers or crostini.

This recipe has gone great with PITAs for centuries . . .

<u>HUMMUS</u>

2 cups canned chick peas (garbanzo beans), drained

2-4 garlic cloves

cumin to taste

6 tablespoons fresh lemon juice

2-4 tablespoons olive oil

3 tablespoons tahini

salt to taste

1/2 cup plain low-fat yogurt

chopped fresh parsley

Purée all ingredients in a food processor. Adjust seasonings, adding more garlic or salt or lemon juice if needed. Serve with... PITAs, of course!

Chapter 7:
Location, Location, Location

<u>Anywhere We Hang Our Towels Is Home</u>

The Bikini Team can commandeer, co-opt, or Lucy-and-Ethel any imaginable space. Take, for example, our move from the Swimming Hole's *Rive Gauche* to its *Rive Droite*. One fine day, we'd just had it with the lack of space for manipulating our chairs on the pool's left bank. Our sun was being blocked by a huge utility fence! Once we made up our minds to mass-migrate, we picked up our armloads of accoutrements and, lickety-split, we shifted locales. That was in the mid-90s. We've occupied our corner of the right bank ever since. We've never looked back.

Because Bikini is a state of mind, the Bikini Team makes the places they choose their own. Claiming space as we do takes almost no practice, just a little chutzpah, a healthy dose of exuberance, and sometimes a bit of dumb luck.

Our Town

By all rights, our readers should know what the Bikini Team is up against in pursuing high life, stylishness, and sophisticated entertainment in a small Southern town like Davidson. You have likely already picked up on hints that our community is challenged by academic stuffiness. You may not have already figured out that the pervasive influence on the town is John Calvin. At this point in Davidson's history, the Methodist Church may have a higher number of members than the college's Presbyterian Church, but Presbyterianism, in all its cultural manifestations, got here first and still reigns supreme. That being the case, the team's penchants for relaxation, horseplay, and fashionable iconography (e.g., jewelry) has caused confusion and met with resistance.

One story explains our challenge. A senior professor at the college wanted to make her mother's final years happy and easy, so she moved her mother to town from the D. C. area. She assumed her mother would be delighted to live with her in her idyllic college town. After three months, however, her mother was packing up to leave, complaining bitterly of boredom and comparing her situation to "living in a convent." We know exactly how this feisty geriatric feels, but we're not going anywhere just yet. Instead, we strive mightily to provide some pizzazz to both town and gown.

Celebrations

When the team hits a public venue, everyone knows we've arrived. This is not only because we are put together and cheerfully boisterous wherever we go, but also because our members are likely to bear distinguishing marks that serve as conversation pieces. One night, for example, we were out celebrating Nancy's birthday at a lovely restaurant in our neighborhood, despite her recent ankle surgery. Her huge cast required that she be taken inside the restaurant in a wheel chair, whereupon she was transferred, with no little exertion on other team members' parts, to a dining chair. She propped up her foot on another chair piled high with pillows. Given the blood-alcohol level of the only unaccompanied man in the establishment, he found that cast remarkably fast. We all waited patiently while he searched his pockets for a pen he could use to sign it. Having executed his signature, he stood back, rocked on his heels, and looked around the table as if he'd just asked one of us to go steady, but couldn't remember exactly *which* one. The team returned to talking among ourselves, all at once, and ignored him until he toddled off.

Later that evening, when it was time to leave, the team wheeled Nancy out of the restaurant and into the parking lot, drenched with October rain. Still talking simultaneously at high volume, the ambulatory team members forgot about putting the brakes on Nancy's wheel chair and lost sight of her as she rolled helplessly into the path of oncoming traffic, had there been any.

Catching sight of her runaway vehicle, two teammates rushed to her rescue and bundled her into the car while others continued to chit-chat. Lina tried, unsuccessfully, to collapse the wheel chair so that it would fit in the back of her station wagon. At her wit's end with the uncooperative wheel chair, she picked it up and, in a move worthy of the Hulk (and expletives befitting a sailor), single-handedly threw it, uncollapsed, in the way-back. That took care of that! Another birthday celebrated.

Galas

The Bikini Team loves galas—so much so that, when in attendance, we tend to take over. Think of it as a benign social terrorism. Galas tap into our *joie de vivre*, and, when we arrive, we look and act plenty *joie*-ful. When we arrive at an opening at a tony gallery, we can be counted on to show up in full goddess regalia, looking ethereal and laying on our admiration for the art.

We associate one place in particular with galas: Cynthia's deck. One year, for the summer solstice party, Cynthia had set her deck magically aglow with candlelight and had decorated with lush summer greenery—the party promised to celebrate the longest day of the year (one of our favorites) in style. Then midsummer madness struck. The temperature, usually steamy during North Carolina's June, plunged into the 50s, chilling the guests to the bone. To warm up, people started drinking wine. The trouble was that some of those people didn't stop. With excess drinking came unwanted lunging. Suffice it to say that one team member had arrived in a new white summer dress and left in a dress the color of merlot. We've decided that Cynthia's deck is the perfect place to continue the solstice parties, but we will make one important change: in the future, we will dispatch unwanted lungers without ado, over the railing.

From Pinot Grigio to Pinot Noir

That deck is also the site of casual get-togethers and suppers before team events. Many of these gatherings are spontaneous; all of them involve libations, whether alcoholic or not. On one particular evening, prior to the team's attending a concert at the local college, a couple of members convened on the deck for a quick salad and a glass of wine. They left the deck and arrived at the concert full of themselves, giggling, and waving to anyone they thought they recognized without their glasses. After an especially raucous fit of laughter, another team member turned to the convivial pair and asked, "Where have you two been? The House of Wine?" The name stuck. We all understand each other when we say we'll begin an evening at our very own "House of Wine."

Other team members' houses carry different associations with celebrations. Cary is famous for her Christmas party, complete with Jay's Bloody Marys. Lina's obsessively neat bungalow hosts various stages in progressive dinners and the occasional Dirty Santa party, just for the team. Ann's house, untidy if Boots has been vacationing, often finds us gathering before a gala or on a Friday afternoon to unwind. Nancy's den boasts the team's largest TV. That's naturally where we convene for our movie nights. Everyone brings something to eat and drink, the Media Specialist picks up the DVD, and we settle in comfortably.

About Townies

When we're out and about town, we're often on Main Street at Summit Coffee. Once upon a time, Summit meetings seemed forever confined to Saturday morning coffee. Then Summit started serving wine and beer on weekends. It's now our "House of Wine" away from home! Summit's interior, perfect for chilly off-season days, is intimate and cozy. Summer permits excursions onto the spacious patio at the rear of the building, where sun umbrellas shield customers from rays during the day and from sudden storms in the evening.

Thursday night is "Townie Night" at Summit. Strictly speaking, townies grew up in Davidson and still live there, but on "Townie Night" anyone in town who's inclined to show up around 8:30 is welcome. We each enjoy a bottled water, a cup of coffee, a glass of wine, or a bottle of beer and swap stories about the day, the week, or, appropriately enough, the town. The crowd shifts from one Thursday to the next, but the core is usually the Bikini Team, their spouses, and their guests.

Lina, a townie to her toes, is in her element at Summit. PITAs clear out! (See Chapter 6.) Although Lina is rarely what anyone could call retiring, she seems unusually emboldened when she arrives on a Thursday evening, orders a glass of Castle Rock pinot noir, and begins unwinding after a long day at "S." Gradually, she sheds the stresses of the past week, loosens up, and, as it were, goes to town critiquing assorted personages without mercy, liberally sprinkling her remarks with a belly laugh that belies the nickname given her by her childhood piano teacher—"Tiny Lina." In her most agitated moments, she pops up from her chair, gesticulates wildly with her arms, and unconsciously shakes her fanny while dressing down someone who has had the misfortune of striking her as an idiot. On Townie Night, Lina may *look* like Doris Day—another of our pet names for her—but she could send Rock Hudson off to hide under the couch.

Retreat and Advance

The Bikini Team retreats at least once a year. Wherever we go, of course, we must be near water, and our bikinis will be tucked in our bags. One member's mountain house, which sits on an exquisite little lake, has been a favorite get-away. It too is equipped with a balcony, lest any of the members lose her cool, become a PITA, and need to be threatened with getting pitched over the railing.

At sunset, the mountains and forest in the distance seem outlined in a halo of light. We often sit out here in the evening, sipping a drink, soaking up the beauty, and cutting up. It was here that, one year, our esteemed CEO, the serene Miss Haley, and the Sergeant-at-Arms, Nancy Gardner, treated the team to its most memorable awards ceremony. The secrecy and suspense surrounding the event were palpable. Our noble leaders solemnly marched onto the deck dressed in togas, wreathed in laurel, and bearing a cardboard box of trophies. Each was inscribed in Latin, lending the illusion of difference in this particular year even as the awards were distributed to the usual suspects.

As always, the CEO and Sergeant-at-Arms shared the Most Valuable Player Award—called, this time around, the "Histrio Pretiosissimus" award. Cary received the trophy for "Carpe Diem"; alas, the MC said that no one this year was eligible for the "Carpe Noctem" award. Cynthia, as usual, was "Tiro Anni," or Rookie of the Year. And Lina, as always, won "Praemium Magnae Linae"—none other than the Big Lina Award. As each teammate came forward to claim her prize, our leaders congratulated her for achieving excellence in the year 2000, a year that saw the Olympics—a fitting background for each team member's *summa cum laude* performance. To Mount Olympus and beyond!

When we return to earth, the Bikini Team is constitutionally incapable of being near a secluded body of water and, at the same time, resisting the urge to remove their uniforms and skinny dip. (The reader may have already noticed a recurring theme in this book regarding the team's passion for this activity.) We always succumb at least once at the mountain retreat. This venture becomes complicated when we are sharing the lake with someone else—especially if they're men—but we always manage to go *au naturel* without being spied or giving offense. (At least, we *think* we do!) The lake water feels indescribable on a hot August day.

The tranquility we value in this venue is subject to the occasional disruption. On one especially frenzied night, just days after the serial bomber Eric Rudolph had escaped into the North Carolina mountains, team members engaged in a game of musical beds that backfired. Although the mountain house has plenty of beds for everyone, team members usually shift around the house at night, trying to find their ideal sleeping space. On the night in question, Lina—who is given not just to "personal summers," but to "personal heat waves"—had been assigned to a hot room and was having trouble falling asleep. (Not to mention the fact that, as Lina is wont to say, Nancy TURNS THE DAMNED AIR-CONDITIONING OFF.) She naturally gravitated to the couch in the living room for relief. Unbeknownst to her, another member, assigned to a room with too many people in it, was seeking solitude when, having arrived nude in the dark living room, she

112

headed for the sofa where, unbeknownst to her, Lina was already sleeping. As the solitude-seeker began to lie down, she put her hands directly on Lina's throat, at which point the startled Lina awoke, screaming that she was being attacked by Eric Rudolph. To this day, team members remain close friends, but are always sure to stay put in separate bedrooms.

Full Circle under the Moon

At the Swimming Hole the Bikini Team was born, and to the Swimming Hole the team inevitably returns. On a warm September night, just after Labor Day and before the pool is covered for the season, a few stealthy, black-clad bodies make their way to the wooded side of the pool, where the security fence is lowest. One reaches over the top of the fence, grabs a chair, and lifts it over to her side. Another reaches over the fence and slides a chair next to the inside of the fence. She stands up on the chair on her side and, ever so gingerly, places one foot on the other chair, momentarily straddling the fence, then lifts her agile body to the chair on the other side, finally reaching the concrete around the baby pool.

The others follow. They avoid the security lights and, they hope, any watchful eyes driving by on the road up the hill. They strip down to their birthday suits, and—silently, joyfully—slip into the cool, still water, barely making a ripple. Every now and then, they look up at the moon, then submerge their heads and let their hair flow sensuously around their faces. They drift peacefully, aimlessly. Thus, they say farewell to the summer.

Chapter 8:
Attitude Check—
Becoming Bikini-able

Few women ask us how to become Bikini-able, but we assume nevertheless that they are dying to know. Although we have no comprehensive system for this process, we offer some scattershot tips.

The single most important ingredient in Bikini-ability, as the preceding pages make abundantly clear, is attitude. Bodily perfection comes only with air-brushing. Bikini Team members believe that true beauty embraces and shines through imperfections, whether those of birth or of aging. Women who wait in the wings, hoping to lose weight, increase muscle tone, or smooth wrinkles before making a public appearance are wasting time! Those issues about body image, although worthy of attention, can be addressed WHILE you live your life.

Once your attitude is based on self-acceptance, the rest is relatively minor. Eating right and exercising regularly are, of course, givens. They also tend to come along with loving the skin you're in.

Body-ability

When it comes to wearing a bikini, most women are most self-conscious about their abs. Working on abs involves some good news. First, it can be done efficiently every day, with sit-ups of one fashion or another. Second, even when you're driving or working out on machines in the gym, keeping your abs tight helps to strengthen them and reduce bulge. Third, as Nancy reminds us often both with words and by example, when you're too busy or forgetful to exercise, a good belly laugh gives those abs a terrific workout!

116

Glutes and ham-strings rate a close second where shyness about revealing our bodies is concerned. Many fairly painless exercises target these areas effectively— for example, the dead-lift, illustrated on a variety of Web sites. Hold a ten-pound weight in each hand and rest your hands, arms extended, at your sides. Lower your upper body (bending at the waist), until your back parallels the floor. Let your arms continue to dangle naturally; the weights will descend in front of your shins. Repeat 15 times or in 2 sets of 10-12.

At the pool, you'll need to stay hydrated. Nothing is worse than lacking cold water or arriving at the pool with a big chunk of ice you can't drink. To avoid these frustrations, freeze a bottle of water almost to the top, then, just as you're heading out the door, top it off with water. The bottle will remain cold during your entire stay at the pool and will melt in sync with your thirst. Lina, whose passion for regimentation has earned her the nickname of "Mrs. Clean," prefers to freeze an entire bottle full of water, then remove it from the freezer and put it on her porch approximately (no, exactly) 48 minutes before leaving the house. The time lapse allows for the right amount of melting.

At home, after a modest supper and during those long hours of lusting after something sweet, we recommend an indulgence that hardly counts (and that won't hurt). Keep a pint of first-rate ice cream in your freezer—Ben and Jerry's, say, or Hagen Daas—and, when the sugar pang hits, nibble 1, 2, or 3 teaspoons full. You can satisfy your craving without over-doing the calories.

Suit-abilty

Buying the right suit is crucial to feeling good about going public, but what works for one woman doesn't work for all. As Bikini Team members testify, deciding on a suit is all about choosing architecture. Each body, however, has its own housing requirements. Bikini Team members shop for uniforms at places as diverse as Target, Victoria's Secret, J. Crew, Nordstrom, and Athleta. One brand that provides underwired tops and bottoms with strategically positioned Spandex (and that's available near us) is Tara Grinna.

For women who are squeamish about transitioning from a one-piece to a two-piece, our CEO and Coach has developed the handy Bikini Adaptor Kit™. It's easy to use and cost-effective (just $9.99), and it helps with those first daring days of exposing the midriff. The kit contains a piece of panty-hose in "Nude," cut to fit around a one-piece in the space that a bikini leaves bare. It creates the illusion of naked flesh while preserving the psychological comfort of full coverage.

The suit, while at center stage, is only the beginning of the BT ensemble, which also includes a cover-up, shoes, hat or visor, and beach bag. We're careful not to over-coordinate, lest we become matchy-matchy. A tee shirt, sarong, summery skimmer-shift, or short skirt can provide admirable covering. Cary made an adorable mini-skirt by cutting open a pair of jeans. The look is distinctly hers. Ann found the perfect beach bag for the team through her Mary Kay representative. It's black vinyl with long, shoulder-friendly straps and a large, clear, flat pocket on one side. We all insert the Bikini Team logo into the see-through pocket and— *voila!*—the bags bear our signature and carry our stuff.

When accessorizing for the pool, the CEO reminds us, remove watches. They leave unsightly tan lines and don't belong on a vacation.

Shoes are functional, but attractive—virtually all manner of sandals and thongs. The flip flops Cynthia's mother found and mailed to her warrant special mention. They may be the most adorable single item of clothing ever produced to reflect the Bikini ethos. Two white-sequined straps traverse the top of the foot. Affixed at the center of the strap closest to the toes is a red bikini bottom with black polka dots, and, attached just above, on other strap, is a matching bikini top. The sandals give the impression that red bikinis with black polka dots are sitting on top of Cynthia's feet. The floating bikini, one of our favorite logos, is right there on ready-made shoes, as if someone had read our collective minds and rushed this must-have design right into production! As covetous as the other Team members were when Cynthia showed off her new acquisition at the pool, everyone was gratified to learn that other pairs could be ordered on line from Collage. (Otherwise, Cynthia's health could have been in serious jeopardy, as the urge to knock her out or knock her off for purposes of shoe-confiscation was intense.)

To make breaking out of the house and heading to the pool as easy and timely as possible, keep your beach bag packed with essentials—sunglasses (reading and otherwise), tissues, pen or pencil, lip gloss, sun screen, and so forth—so that you need to add only items like cell phone, car keys, water bottle, and fresh towel.

Switching out suits will introduce the annoyance of tan lines. Some tips to minimize this inconvenience include beginning the season with your skimpiest bottom, so that, from that point forward, you'll be tan for all occasions. Also slip out of the straps to your top whenever you can (halter tops usually excepted!) so that you won't have noticeable strap lines. Remember to be careful about newly exposed skin, which can burn, hurt, and look terrible, thus defeating the whole purpose of lying out in the first place. Cover those tender, vulnerable areas with # 30 sunscreen, and be sure to use some form of sunscreen on every part of your body. The skin on the neck and chest areas is thinner than that on your arms and legs, so take extra care with it.

Your face has the most delicate skin of all, and many of the sunscreens that work on the rest of your body will irritate your face. Many lotions on the market contain #15 sunscreen; they both moisturize and protect. Most cosmetic companies make excellent, gentle sunscreens specifically for the face. Facial sunscreen should be worn daily. Also watch for warning signs on your skin—changed moles, for instance—and consult your doctor about the least worry.

Float-ability

The single most important piece of any Bikini Team member's equipment is the float, which enables her to endure the worst of summer's heat while basking atop the cool water. At one time, we all used the inexpensive, plastic floats that take hours to inflate and require massive lungs (we eventually gave up and took the floats to Wayne Stowe's Exxon station). These were, on just about all counts, a nuisance. They were very difficult to mount, too easy to deflate, too big to store, and, perhaps most offensive, unattractive. Most of them were solid-color neon—yellow, pink, or green.

One was covered in multi-color indentations resembling those on a muffin tin—hence the owner's nickname, "Cupcake."

Then one spring, we discovered the float that was to revolutionize our days at the Swimming Hole. Target began to carry a mesh float that stays on top of the water by virtue of an inflated perimeter rim and pillow for the head. The inflation time is thus radically reduced from the old float—to about two minutes. Deflation is equally quick, and, once deflated, the float folds in on itself into an almost flat circle, thanks to its flexible metal rim. The collapsed float can then be stashed in a mesh, zippered carrying bag. Even if the float is still wet at that point, it will dry through the mesh. The real advantage of this float is that the mesh, which allows water through, helps us stay cool on very hot days (and even days when the water has warmed up almost as much as the air). In addition to their practicality, these floats are aesthetically superior to their precursors. The colors are attractive and soothing. Cary's even has a poignant picture of an island hut tucked beneath billowy cumulae—which, because they are pictured on the pillow, always enable her to have her head in the clouds.

These floats are subject to two flaws that we would correct if we could reach out to manufacturers. One is that they don't have a drink holder—a relatively minor inconvenience, except when one of our admirers plays cabaña boy of the day and brings us fresh-squeezed lemonade to sip while we float. The other deficiency is more serious: the float's center, which lacks support (just where we need it most), tends to dip down into the water. This state of affairs is unacceptable. In order to tan, our midriffs must be above water! Bikini Team ingenuity being what it is, however, we have developed a solution: the noodle. Each member places one or two noodles to support the float underneath her derrière. A weird look, but effective. We all agree that if the float's manufacturer would place another inflatable band where we now place the noodles, the product would approach perfection.

Mounting, dismounting, and turning over are all skills that expert floaters have mastered. The mount is especially tricky, although it can be gracefully accomplished in two ways. The first is to get into the water with the float, then hoist your body onto the float, almost as if you were getting out of the pool. Only a belly-down mount should be attempted in this manner; when a bottom-down attempt results in the float's slipping away out from under your tush, you feel (not to mention look) klutzy, and rightly so. The other mount involves putting the float into the water and then carefully placing your body onto it from the edge of the pool. Because our floats are lightweight, this mount causes them to look as if they're sinking—but only for a moment. When the float's buoyancy takes over and restores equilibrium to your float and you, you may appear to others to have executed a thing of beauty—the veritable equivalent of a swan dive. You can then safely secure your noodles and lie back, soaking up the sun while staying refreshed.

Readers should be warned that trying to mount a float in any other way than the two described here may have disastrous consequences, the worst being unseemly awkwardness on the order of a giraffe having slipped on a banana. This, as some of us well remember, elicits guffaws from teammates. You are advised to make extra trips to the pool outside official meeting hours to perfect this essential maneuver.

Dismounting isn't nearly as big a deal. Swivel your rear 90 degrees until your legs are bent at the knee and your feet dangle in the water. Hold on to the rim of the float with your hands and gently lift it off of your fanny as you stand up in the pool. If you've had a rough mount, dismounting well can save some face.

Turning over is nearly as challenging as mounting, yet turn over we must in order to do the difficult back work. (No one ever said team sports were easy!) The objective is to move as little as possible and thus create minimal disturbance and disequilibrium on your float. Do not try rolling over as you would in bed—you haven't enough space. You must turn yourself over without going anywhere, a feat at any age, for any gender, and at any level of physical prowess. Your forearms and elbows can do the lion's share of the work. Use them to prop yourself up—only slightly, lest you rock the float—then ease your body into a half-circular turn. Make it your purpose not to move your body to the right or the left; it must remain stationary while you change positions. There ya go—bottoms up!

To return to your original, face-up position, reverse the above process, using the underside of your forearms to lift your chest, rather than your back. Keep practicing—if we can become adept at these moves, anyone can!

On cooler days, when you don't have to stay wet to keep cool, try basting—dipping in and out of the water, then returning to your lounge chair—as needed.

One Woman's Journey to Nirvana—The Four Stages of Bikini Awareness

1. At age two, I noticed my bathing suit was larger than my brother's. It covered my stomach and chest. I was perplexed by this injustice. I vowed to right this wrong.

2. At age sixteen, I saw a *Playboy Magazine* article entitled "Bridget Bardot at 40." I was inspired. I vowed to age as gracefully as Bridget.

3. At age 40, I noticed the other women at the pool were wearing one-piece Suits of Shame. I vowed to save them.

4. At age 50, I float serenely on a raft. My true friends surround me. My imaginary friends take care of my mundane responsibilities. My suit is a lot smaller than my brother's or my husband's. My Bikini state of mind has taken me to Nirvana. I vow to stay.

Chapter 9:
The Bikini Male

Our Better Third

Although Bikini Team members find fulfillment by playing hard and working hard, we realize our lives would be incomplete without males. We love men, and we accept them, despite their weaknesses, because we understand their importance. We recognize, for example, that our beautiful offspring would not exist were it not for the contributions of the males in our lives. We also understand that living with a goddess can be a challenge for most men, who, being mortal, need our patience and kindness. In other words, we are not male-bashers. We do not have Earl in the trunk.

Female Blinders

When we gather at the pool, our energy and focus are directed toward the team. We tend to ignore those around us, males and females, in order to concentrate on our talk and tanning. Once at Townie Night, a male member of the pool recognized one of our members (who was not in uniform at the time). Although she had not seen him before, he mentioned to her that he had seen that group of women who gather daily near the diving board. After confessing he had performed jackknives and swan dives in order to attract our attention, he asked, "Did you see me?" The Bikini Team member responded, a little sheepishly, "Well, no." She politely explained that we had important business to discuss when we were there, but she assured him that we would applaud his performance at the next meeting.

The Male Species

In order to help clarify dialogue at our meetings, we find it advantageous to have various classifications of the males in our lives. These classifications are not meant to restrict the type of men we encounter, but labeling gives us a better understanding of the opposite sex. These categories may help you understand the importance of the male as a complement to the Bikini Team member's identity.

The Maintenance Man

This label is not limited to males who assist around the house, help carpool the kids to soccer games, or mow the lawn and spread the fertilizer. What's more, this label does not include a male who is a high maintenance person himself.

For anyone on the team who might be single, the Maintenance Man is someone who helps the teammate find and complete her sexual identity—with no emotional strings attached, unless we want them. (Think James Taylor—"Come-a, come-a, come-a, come-a, come come"). Several members have found that the Maintenance Man might visit once a week, perhaps as a "Sunday night regular." He may be a landscaper who tends to a Bikini Goddess's trunk and limbs, an electrician who can recharge her battery, or any uncomplicated man who is good with his hands. Although some women might find this particular kind of relationship awkward (and our Chaplain consistently frowns on it), we acknowledge that this kind of man is at times both necessary and fun.

The Real Maintenance Man

Our local service station owner, Wayne Stowe, is our real maintenance man. On any given day in the summer, you can spot four to six Bikini Team cars in his garage. We rely on Wayne for blowing up our old-fashioned rafts (our state of the art rafts don't require Wayne's attention) and our tires. When Lina's daughter accidentally left her laptop in her car, Lina simply called Wayne and asked him to lock the computer in the trunk of her car. Another member recently wrote him a thank you note for all of his help with brakes, ignitions, transmissions, and clutches. Although we write him checks for the work on the cars, he used to blow up the rafts for free (and misses them!). When we make a movie of this book, we hope James Garner will play his part.

The Bikini Team Prototype Husband

We have searched far and wide for this one, but only two men qualify: Jay and Shaw.

Quentin

This is the label we use for all of our former husbands. Although we don't feel excessive anger and resentment toward these men, we understand that their loss is our gain. As a matter of fact, one of our members made the remarkable discovery that all of our ex-husbands are the same person. Indeed, we have come to suspect that all of the ex-husbands in the world are the same person. We know that this hypothesis must be true because we have never seen them all together in the same room at the same time. Thus we refer to these combined males as "Quentin." We do look upon Quentin with some pity, realizing how foolish he was to leave Mount Olympus in order to escape the power and aura of the Bikini Team woman. Ann once sent each of us a generic e-mail to forward to Quentin. If you find it helpful, you may copy and paste.

Memo to Quentin

Dear Quentin,

You blew it. You had it all—a wonderful family, a loving wife, beautiful kids, a great home—and now you are all alone. You are pathetic. You are either moving into or moving out of a small condo, eating frozen food for dinner, and trying to rationalize looking into on-line dating. You probably don't even know what went wrong. What were you thinking? Were you thinking? If you feel like you need help, click on the website below:

<u>www.BikiniTherapy.org</u>

Have a nice day!

Sincerely,

(insert your own name here)

A Quentin sighting is sometimes a topic of discussion at our meetings, but we usually cover this topic under "old business," and we rarely get that far on our crowded agenda.

The Boy Toy

This name applies to the thirty-something male who languishes at the well manicured feet of Bikini Team members. Although young and naïve, the Boy Toy understands how fortunate he is to be in the company of the Bikini Team. Once we invited a Boy Toy to join us at a local bar, and we assured him that he would be surrounded by 255 years of beauty. He was most appreciative, explaining that being with us drew other desirable women to him. The Boy Toy-Bikini Team member relationship is most like a mentor-mentee relationship. And remember, we are all teachers, so we perform well in this role. "God bless you please, Mrs. Robinson."

Wannabe Partners

Some of the men who observe our meetings at the pool are curious about the Bikini Team. They frequently inquire about us, and we don't think it is because they want to see if their wives are potential members. The husband of a local wannabe once said that he would "like to be a mosquito" on one of our towels to hear our discussions. Standing close enough to overhear the remark, his wife responded, "I bet you would." We all knew what he meant.

Our Male Children

These are the most fabulous men in the world. The list includes Forrest, Jake, Hal, Tate, Curtis, Jason, Blake, and baby Lucas. Their mothers are goddesses: need we say more?

Mr. Ab

One of the pool managers during our meetings in the late '90's was named Mr. Rabb, but we affectionately called him Mr. Ab. This name fit, shall we say? He was proud to have us at his pool and missed us on cloudy days. He helped us with our photo shoots and lovingly put our chairs (which we always move to face the sun) back in the boring line-up along the side of the pool. He helped us with our first calendar, and he even offered to store our rafts (the tanning bed) in the bathhouse. Always protective of the team's space, he thought our area of the pool deck ought to be roped off to keep out invaders and wannabes. Although our pool managers are now college students (and fabulous females), we are always in search of another Mr. Ab, our own version of "Mr. Goodbar."

The "I'd love to see that calendar" Male

This type of man usually falls in the senior citizen category. Although his enthusiasm about our work is real and focused, we don't take his compliments seriously. We sometimes encounter this type of man at our local post office (when we are out of uniform). After he says hello and notices our tan, the next remark will be something like, "How can I get a look at that calendar?"

One of our favorites

Lord Bobby, man about town, is one of our favorite locals. On numerous occasions he has offered his private pool for our calendar photo shoot. One summer we decided to accept. When we arrived, he was busy cleaning out the storm debris from the pool so it would look pretty for the photos. After vacuuming the pool, he brought us a bottle of fine wine and six glasses, including one for our team photographer. He is now our self-proclaimed "Cabaña Boy," and he definitely deserves a copy of that calendar. We are thinking of creating an award in his honor, but we don't know exactly what the title will be. We do know that it will include the word "sexy."

The Offensive Male

A student of Ann's once said, "Men. Can't live with 'em, can't shoot 'em."

We really don't know many men we don't like; sometimes when we are out socially, however, we encounter men who assume we are trolling just because they are. These men are Cling-ons who invade our personal space. Although they sometimes make us feel uncomfortable, we never let on. Instead, we respond to questions with prepared scripts. When a Cling-on asks us where we are from, we reply, in unison, "Davidson." One of these offensive males used the tackiest pick-up scheme when he took a pair of a team member's eye-glasses, put them on, squinted, and announced, "Our glasses are exactly alike except that I'm nearsighted and you're farsighted. And you know what they say— opposites attract." Yikes.

Another time, when we were at a local eating establishment on the lake, a young man with spiked hair told us we were beautiful babes. We were polite, but didn't engage in a prolonged conversation because we were afraid he might use his hair as a weapon.

Pitiful Males

Some men we can only pity, like the man we met one night at a local restaurant. One of our members arrived early, and while she was waiting for her teammates, the man moved near her, leaned in closely and whispered, "Hey, Baby. You look lonely. I'm lonely, too. Let's be lonely together." Our teammate sympathetically responded, "Are you insane?"

Bikini Team Husbands

We currently have two married women on our team, and we would like to pay a small tribute to their husbands. These men join us at times for galas and parties, but the strongest contribution they make to the team is understanding how important team membership is to their wives. When Cary tried to relinquish her family membership at the pool, Jay insisted, "No, Cary. You need it!" Shaw and Jay join us for meetings on particularly hot days, but they always keep their heads stuck in their books and give us the space we need and want.

A dear friend of Ann's taught her the ultimate secret of a happy marriage, and Ann has, in turn, taught this secret to Shaw. We will now reveal the secret to you. (Male readers, pull out your palm pilots and type this in.) The secret is "treat your wife like a queen and she will be happy." It is such a simple rule, it is easy to learn, and it works every time.

Daddies

All the members of the Bikini Team are mothers, and therefore we have had some experience with fathers. We have discovered that these men share some traits. Most of the daddies we know have "daddy ears." These men learn to sleep through the night only a few days after a new baby comes home, and they continue to have selective hearing throughout the rest of the child-rearing years. We have also realized that Daddies have unusual eyes. When one of our children can't locate a missing article, we ask, "Did you give a daddy look or a mommy look?" A daddy look is simply a gaze over the surface of the table or desk or toy box, while a mommy look involves moving things around until she comes up with the missing article.

Professional Males

The Bikini Team has several male friends to contact for professional help or political favors. We know it is important to maintain these relationships for health and happiness. One of these is our official Team Photographer, who helps us with our photo shoots for the calendar. We have had several photographers, but we recently needed to search for a new one. After several offers and careful interviewing, we engaged a new Team Photographer who captures our personalities through the eyes of the lens. Of course, the new digital technology has helped, but we appreciate Bill for his work. When we asked Bill how long he could stay during our last photo shoot, he responded, "I could do you all day!" And after a particularly sexy shot of all of our legs dangling in the pool, Bill proudly exclaimed, "That's art!"

We also have a solid (but complicated) relationship with our town's occasional Mayor Pro Tem. Although his real name is John Woods, to us he is the dignified Jean de Bois. Jean de Bois understands that we are important to his political future, so he cultivates a relationship with every member of the team. Once he nominally hosted a "Tree Wake Gala" at his home and asked us to create the most perfect evening. We planned and provided for the party by sending invitations, buying food, and offering entertainment. The gathering celebrated the end of the life of a gigantic maple tree in his front yard.

We dressed as goddesses and mingled with the humans. Jean de Bois, signifying his humility, hosted the party attired in a tuxedo jacket and boxer shorts.

On a serious note, we want to pay tribute to our team doctor, Ed Stubbs. Dr. Stubbs, the gynecologist for most of the team members, was killed in a car accident in the spring of 2003. He was a devoted father, husband, and doctor. Since much of our discussion at the pool centers on hot flashes (we call them "personal summers"), hormone replacement therapy, the benefits of tofu, and our missing organs, the name of our official team doctor came up often. Each of us talked with Dr. Stubbs about the team when we had our annual checkups, and he enjoyed our humor and relished his title. He always noticed the progress of our tans, and he offered to make new "gowns" that included a bikini top. Cynthia shared the calendar with him at her annual checkup. He is the only man we know who has seen five members of the Bikini Team in their bathing suits and their birthday suits. We really miss you, Dr. Stubbs.

If we shadows have offended . . .

Males of all shapes, sizes, and ages are important parts of our lives. Although we may sound negative at times, we certainly don't mean to offend. We know that, with proper training (see Chapter 2), males can compete with us, love us, and respect us—even though they insist on wearing one-piece bathing suits. And as Big Daddy (Nancy's father, Ann's father-in-law) once said, "The good Lord knew what he was doing when he made us incomplete without each other."

* *

F.O.B.T. ("Friends of the Bikini Team")

Male Testimonials:

Richard, age 60-something, the local Y, a. k. a. "Abs of Titanium"

"I know this book will be a best seller, especially if it has pictures. Once these women grab hold of an idea, it's real. They run with it; it gets done."

Pat, age 42, the Swimming Hole

"The Bikini Team—what shall I say? They are definitely Bikini She-ites or Babe Qaeda."

Patrick, age 21, Davidson College student

"The Bikini Team is a collection of extremely attractive women who could pass for 20 years old despite being just a few years older than that."

George, age 47, Nogales, Arizona

"The Bikini Team represents the best of the world: strength and art. Here are five independent women who show strength in their families, their careers, and their friendships. The Bikini Team is art. Ask any man, the most beautiful work of art in the universe is the form of the woman. These Bikini Team women are creations of pure beauty. As a friend and as a man, I thank the Bikini Team for their strength."

David, 50-something, Charlotte, NC

"These women are goddesses. When I look at them, I'm glad I'm a man!"

Mr. Ab, age 30-something, former pool manager, Davidson

"When I was manager, the pool may have opened at 10:00 a.m., but it didn't truly come to life until the Bikini Team arrived in full force and took their place in the team's self-designated official meeting place in the southwest corner of the pool deck. They didn't

announce their presence, but everyone knew they were there."

Tim, age 27, owner of Summit Coffee, Davidson

"The Bikini Team is not entirely about skin and strings, although judging by annual photo spreads it involves plenty of that. The Bikini Team is about spirit. It is women celebrating womanhood. It is friends celebrating friendship. And yet it is also simply a group of women who designate summer months for chatting, tanning, napping, and partying. A novel concept indeed."

John Woods—alias Jean de Bois—ageless, occasional Mayor Pro Tem, Davidson

"When I think of the fabric of the community, the fabric of the community is like the clingings of chlorine holding together supple curves and mounds of the community— and holding the community together in a wonderful and loving yet sensuous sort of way."

(We sometimes have this effect on otherwise articulate, clear-headed men.)

Clint, age 75, former Mayor of Carmel

"These women make my day."

Ralph, 52, Davidson

"Davidson has been born anew—women of life! With or without bikinis, they are the 'pulse,' the female inspiration of Davidson."

Bill, 40-something, the local Y

"I really admire your team and the strong social activism. You women have bigger cajones than any man I know because you teach in the public 'S.' Every day you face that challenge."

Zach, age 40-something, Ann's gardener and imaginary friend

"If you give these women lots of nurturing and care, they will blossom and produce. They require full sun and plenty of water. Avoid shade."

Deepak, age unknown, the Swimming Hole

"Bikini Is a State of Mind . . . this could be bigger than yoga."

Recipes for Chapter 9

Ah, men, the recipes say it all . . .

<u>BEER BUTT CHICKENS</u>

1 whole chicken

juice of a lemon

1 tablespoon paprika

2 teaspoons chili powder

2 teaspoons of cinnamon

1 teaspoon salt

1 teaspoon oregano

1/4 teaspoon cayenne

1/2 teaspoon garlic powder

1 tablespoon Creole seasoning

1 12-ounce can of beer

2 cloves garlic, peeled and smashed

Squeeze lemon juice inside and outside of chicken. Combine paprika, chili powder, oregano, salt, cayenne, garlic powder, cinnamon, and Creole seasoning. Rub inside and outside of chicken. Pour out (or drink) 1/2 can of beer. Add garlic to remaining beer. Insert beer can into chicken's butt. Set chicken on the grill using the 1/2 full beer can as the base (beer can goes into the cavity of the chicken and the chicken sits upright on beer can). Grill for 2 hours on low to medium heat (best if done on the side of grill without the heat source, while the other side is set on low to medium.) When chicken is done, carefully remove can. Let chicken rest for 15 minutes before cutting into pieces.

BOIL THAT CHICKEN.

Fill a large (12-quart is good) canning kettle with water and bring to a rolling boil. Place one whole cleaned chicken into the boiling water. When the water stops boiling, take the chicken out. Cover the pot and when the water comes to a rolling boil again, place the chicken back in the pot. When it comes back to a rolling boil, cover, turn off the burner, leave the chicken in the pot and the pot on the burner. After one hour, the chicken is done. Carefully remove and place on a platter to cool. Debone the chicken and tear the meat into small strips. Place on a large platter. Clean 2 bunches of green onions and split each onion down the middle. Cut in

½-inch pieces and sprinkle over the chicken along with 1 tablespoon soy sauce, 1 tablespoon sesame oil and 2 tablespoons salt. Heat ¼ cup peanut oil until smoking and pour over all. Toss and serve.

SKEWERED CHICKEN

3 whole chicken breasts, boned, skinned and cut into 1-inch cubes

6 scallions (white parts only), cut into 1-inch lengths

Marinade

1/2 cup Japanese soy sauce

1/4 cup sweet sake or sherry

1 teaspoon grated fresh ginger

1 teaspoon sugar

1/4 cup water

Combine marinade ingredients in small saucepan, bring to a boil and simmer one minute. Cool. If using wooden skewers, soak them in water for about half an hour. Thread skewers, alternating scallion and meat. Place skewers and cooled marinade into a large ziplock bag and marinate in the fridge for an hour or two. Grill 4 to 5 minutes on each side, basting often, until crisp and brown.

Bikini Team husbands' recipes . . .

JAY'S BLOODY MARYS

Taste often because you may need more vodka.

vodka

1 jug vegetable juice cocktail (may use spicy hot)

1 jug clamato

vodka

horseradish (freshly ground to taste—the more, the better)

juice of 3 limes

juice of 1 lemon

vodka

Old Bay seasoning (to taste)

Worcestershire sauce (to taste—several glugs)

freshly ground pepper (to taste)

celery salt (to taste)

Taste and add more of anything (to taste).

<u>SHAW'S RECIPE</u>

Who wants Jack Daniels? or W.W.J.D.?

1 ounce Jack Daniels

1 brandy snifter

Pour Jack Daniels into brandy snifter. Heat in microwave for 20 seconds. Swirl, sniff, and enjoy.

Chapter 10:
The Bikini Team Trilogy

Outline of a series of three films that chronicle the lives of The Bikini Team Members

<u>*Episode One, The Ghosts of Summers Past*</u>

Summers, 1960 - 1972

The pool is built, a glistening oasis in a small Southern town.

It becomes the gathering spot for a group of young girls.

The young teammates swim, play Marco Polo, and observe the salient contrast between a woman from California who wears a bikini and all the other ladies in their dark, skirted bathing suits.

The teammates discover boys, fall in love, and prepare

to leave for college and life.

All plans, hopes, and dreams are discussed at the pool.

Episode Two, The Ghosts of Summers Present

Summers, 1990 - 2010

Years later, the teammates return from various places to their hometown and are reunited at the pool.

They raise children, create homes, create art, teach students, make political and financial decisions, and do their best to save the world.

Their children, husbands, and parents swirl around them.

They all grow older.

Their children grow up and they leave home.

Some of their husbands do not grow up, and they leave home.

Fortunately, the good ones stay.

Their parents age and need constant care.

All plans, hopes, and dreams are discussed at the pool.

Episode Three, The Ghosts of Summers Yet to Come

Summers, 2025 - 2035

The teammates age gracefully.

They retire from their pesky day jobs.

They continue to raise children, create homes, create art, teach the young, make political and financial decisions, and try to save the world.

But now they have more time to travel.

They move to the Pines Retirement Community.

They refer to their lives at the Pines as their time "On Golden Pool."

They battle disease and death.

All plans, hopes, and dreams are discussed at the pool.

Suggested actresses to play the parts of the teammates

	Episode One	*Episode Two*	*Episode Three*
Lina	Reese Witherspoon	Doris Day	Tina Turner
Cary	Jessica Simpson	Meg Ryan	Katharine Hepburn
Cynthia	Angelina Jolie	Ashley Judd	Sophia Loren
Nancy	Katie Holmes	Holly Hunter	Nancy Gardner
Ann	Uma Thurman	Madonna	Catherine Deneuve

Other suggestions

	Episode One	Episode Two	Episode Three
Big Lina	Bridget Bardot	Gloria Steinem	
Jay		Ed Harris	Robert Duval
Shaw	Bruce Springsteen	Sean Connery	Paul Newman
Jean de Bois	Clay Aiken	Martin Sheen	
Wayne Stowe		James Garner	
Quentin		Jack Nicholson	

Extras for crowd scenes

Brad Pitt, Johnny Depp, George Clooney, Lance Armstrong, Nicholas Cage, Antonio Banderas, Kevin Costner, Arnold Schwarzenegger, Denzel Washington, Gerard Depardieu, Woody Allen

Note: Work is progressing on a second trilogy

Tentative Titles:

Episode Four, The Life Support Years
Episode Five, Four Funerals and a Wedding
Episode Six, The Next Life

Recipes for Chapter 10

Episode 1: We didn't know it at the time, but this was our first experience with the perfect food marriage . . .

POTATO CHIPS WITH MAYO AND CREAM CHEESE

Mix enough mayo into some softened cream cheese until you have a dip-able consistency. Dip and enjoy on your best friend's back porch after a day spent at the pool.

Episode 2: Salad days . . . we grew up, and thankfully our tastes changed . . .

OLIVES AND FETA

In a beautiful bowl or platter mix together a variety of Mediterranean olives (pits in) and chunks of good quality feta cheese. Use your fingers and enjoy. Perfect with a glass of zinfandel. RED, of course.

Episode 3: Winter of life . . .

PRUNE CAKE

1-1/2 cups pitted, chopped prunes

1-1/2 cups sugar

3/4 cup shortening

3 eggs, beaten

2-3/4 cups all purpose flour

1/2 teaspoon salt

1 teaspoon mace

1 teaspoon cinnamon

1-1/2 teaspoons baking soda

3/4 cup boiling, strong coffee

Cream together sugar and shortening. Fold in beaten eggs. Add prunes. Mix 1/2 teaspoon baking soda with the spices, and mix the other teaspoon soda with the hot coffee. Sift the flour and spice mixture together, then fold into batter. Add the boiling coffee and mix well. Pour into 3 layer tins that have been generously greased and floured. Bake at 375 degrees for 25 minutes. Cool and frost with your favorite cream cheese frosting.

Epilogue:
The Mosquito on the Towel

"It's not if you can, it's if you will," affirm the goddesses. But those of us who aren't official members of the Bikini Team might also venture to say that a bit of predisposition is necessary, too. Let's face it; some of us just aren't Bikini material. Maybe the Training Regime is too daunting, or the shady spot under a big umbrella is more appealing, or you're a man, or, alas, the meetings fall right in the middle of prime office hours. Some of us might not even want to be BT material. Heck, some of us might not even want to be associated with the Bikini Team and its philosophies.

But take it from me, one whose bikini encounters have been so up close and personal that the towel-lounging mosquitoes are envious: even if we've resigned ourselves to ruffled one-pieces, this book is still undeniably valuable. Why? Because each of us has something to glean from these wild women and their mantras of self-love, friendship, and teamwork. Besides, even if we aren't Bikini-able, chances are we know someone who *is*. Goddesses are all around us. It may be a co-worker or boss, or that sixth-grade teacher you never could quite get a handle on. It may be a sibling or a close friend. You may live with a closeted Bikini Babe. You may even be married to one. Do not pass off her strange behavior as "erratic" or "nutso." She may just be struggling to let her true Bikini identity emerge. That's where this checklist comes in handy.

Fifteen Signs That Someone You Know Is Bikini Team Material

1. Seasonally Affected Mood Disorder: Cloudy day = lots of pouting.
2. She's mowing the yard . . . in a Brazilian cut.
3. She flies to Costa Rica for dental work.

4. Flies back for check-ups.

5. Mysterious disappearances every day between 11:00 a.m. and 4:00 p.m.

6. You vacation to Italy. Only souvenir your mother requests is a blue bikini.

7. She knows the latest gossip two days before you do. Or, more accurately, two days before it happens.

8. A shrine to the summer solstice is prominently displayed somewhere in her home.

9. She vehemently opposes year-round schooling.

10. She buckles a neon orange inflatable raft into the passenger seat of her black truck.

11. You suspect that she might have an imaginary housekeeper.

12. She goes to the tanning bed to "practice."

13. The only people who might laugh louder than she does are her closest friends.

14. You hear, on more than one occasion, someone say to her, "It's so strange to see you with all your clothes on!"

15. She calls herself a goddess . . . and you believe her.

THE AUTHORS

L to R: Cynthia, Lina, Nancy, Ann

About the authors

<u>Nancy Gardner</u> is called the Energizer Bunny by her colleagues at work. At 27 years of age (she started counting down at the age of 40), she still feels youthful in her bikini. An avid runner and Y member, she does her best ab workout during the Bikini Team "tanning bed" sessions when team members put their floats together, laze in the pool, and laugh till it hurts.

<u>Ann Haley</u> is the founder, chief executive officer, and coach of the Bikini Team. She has spent countless hours developing and perfecting the extremely precise and demanding Bikini Team Spring Training Regime. Coach Haley leads the Team through this program each spring, ensuring that members will be physically, emotionally, and spiritually prepared for the rigorous season of tanning and relaxing ahead.

<u>Cynthia Lewis</u> is a professor of English and a non-fiction writer. As the newest member of the Bikini Team, she annually wins "Rookie of the Year" at the Awards Ceremony. She aspires to "Player of the Year."

<u>Lina Soares</u>—or "Mrs. Clean," as she is known on the Bikini Team—is a teacher of the gifted and a doctoral student in curriculum instruction. She tears herself away from "powering down"—vacuuming, mowing the grass, and herding dust bunnies—to attend Bikini Team meetings faithfully.

Printed in the United States
55308LVS00001B/48